THE BIG BOOK OF SIX SIGMA TRAINING GAMES

Creative Ways to Teach Basic DMAIC Principles and Quality Improvement Tools

Chris Chen

Hadley Roth

McGraw-Hill

New York   Chicago   San Francisco
Lisbon   London   Madrid   Mexico City   Milan
New Delhi   San Juan   Seoul   Singapore
Sydney   Toronto

The McGraw·Hill Companies

1 2 3 4 5 6 7 8 9 0   FGR/FGR   0 9 8 7 6 5 4

ISBN 0-07-144385-1

 This book is printed on recycled, acid-free paper containing a minimum of 50% recycled de-inked paper.

CONTENTS

Contents

Introduction

The Big Book of Six Sigma Games was conceived to help you convey the practical wisdom of Six Sigma to others in an enjoyable, energetic, and insightful format. While some of the concepts of Six Sigma can be intimidating (especially statistics!), we've created a resource of games, exercises, and instruments that will help put Six Sigma in a context that can be readily understood and applied.

The games are designed to create a rich learning experience for participants with varying degrees of Six Sigma knowledge. The debriefings and group discussions are flexible enough to address the various Six Sigma experience levels of all participants appropriately. Whether you are training novices, Green Belts, or Black Belts, these games will help keep your training sessions fresh and your participants energized.

Don't be misled by the word *games* in the title of this book. While the exercises are designed to be fun and entertaining games, they are also powerful learning experiences. They incorporate the principles of experiential learning that help participants understand, internalize, and retain information and principles better than traditional teaching methods.

While some games typically associated with Six Sigma concepts (such as Deming's famous "red bead" exercise) require specialized equipment to facilitate, we've designed all of the exercises in this book so that they can be performed with common, everyday materials. Using playing cards, water, newspapers, and other readily available items, you'll be able to explore and demonstrate all of the insights and learning points that make Six Sigma so powerful.

The games are organized in a simple, easy to use construct of chapters based on the Define, Measure, Analyze, Improve, and Control (DMAIC) principles familiar to Six Sigma practitioners. Each chapter includes facilitator primers on the concepts illustrated by the games in that chapter. We've also included discussion questions and facilitator notes to prime the debrief exercises and guide participant learning. However, as you gain experience with the exercises, we believe you will find many new and different ways to apply them in your Six Sigma efforts.

We have chosen not to include such classic exercises as "Helicopter" and "Red Bead" in this book. They are widely used to teach quality initiative concepts and are readily available in the public domain.

HOW TO USE THIS BOOK

Each game has the following construct:

- *Reference Title* Use this title to give you and your participants a common way to refer to each game.

- *Descriptive Title* Each game also has a descriptive title (in parentheses after the reference title), which describes the main learning point or process the game is designed to demonstrate. Use this to focus your efforts to select a game.

- *Description* A short description of the design of the game. Use this to get a quick understanding of how the game is designed and how it might meet the needs of your audience.

- *Purpose* A list of the learning points typically demonstrated by the game. Use this to select a game that is well suited to the needs of your audience.

- *Time Required* We have provided estimated times required to run each exercise to assist you with planning your training. These are estimates based on our experience and can vary significantly based on local needs and circumstances.

- *Number of Participants* The minimum and maximum number of participants suggested for effective use of each exercise. While these are generally not hard-and-fast limits, we suggest you understand an exercise thoroughly before going outside these guidelines.

- *Materials Required* A list of materials required to run each exercise. This list should be reviewed while planning your exercise. Most of the materials are normal office supplies, but some might require a trip to the store.

- *Process* The step-by-step instructions, which in many cases include verbatim scripts to be read to participants. We suggest you follow the process steps exactly as written until you have gained enough experience with an exercise to customize it to your needs.

- *Discussion Questions* These are suggested questions to use during your debrief. While they cover many of the points typically experienced by participants, they are not comprehensive. You can, and should, add discussion questions based on your local circumstances and needs.

- *Facilitator Notes* These are the tips we offer from our own experience to help you run each exercise smoothly and effectively. They may also include insight regarding how participants typically react during an exercise or alternative designs to emphasize certain learning points.

WEB RESOURCES

Resources to support your training (handouts, data sets, statistical tools, etc.) are available at *http://books.mcgraw-hill.com/training/download*. The following icon indicates that electronic versions of resources from this book are available:

HOW TO FACILITATE

Trust the process. Each game is a proven construct for accomplishing its specified purpose. Follow the game instructions carefully, especially the first few times you run the game. Even if you aren't sure at times where the participants are heading in their discussions and actions, the process will guide them to the correct learning points.

Be open to unexpected outcomes and unanticipated learning points. Listen carefully and be ready to grasp each "teachable moment" that presents itself. Human interaction during these games is dynamic, and participants who are engaged and focused find many ways to learn.

Stay on pace. The games are fun and engaging and sometimes it is tempting to let a game run long and shortchange the time available for the debriefing. We strongly encourage you to avoid this situation. Much of the learning occurs and is solidified in the debriefing. The discussion questions in each exercise reinforce points already perceived by participants and bring out new learning points through group observation and discussion. We generally allow at least as much time for discussion after the exercise as we do for the exercise itself.

Be prepared. Because of the nature of the content, some of the games in this book are somewhat more complex than typical team-building games, particularly the games dealing with statistics and measurement. For these games, the facilitator should thoroughly understand the concepts being demonstrated and should also be sensitive to how much background the participants have in statistics.

Emphasize that the participants are responsible for their own learning. As a facilitator, you cannot make someone else learn. You can only help create the opportunity to learn. One of the primary reasons games appeal to learners is that they allow participants to bring their personal experiences and insights to the table. The game, or experiential learning, construct can also result in a broader application of learning. The key point is that because participants develop the learning experience themselves through game participation, they own it and the responsibility for their learning.

Encourage all participants to be "learning partners." All participants have insights and knowledge that other participants can learn from. Encourage them to share their insights and to be open to learning from others. The experiential learning principles designed into each game in this book will facilitate the process of participants learning from each other.

ACKNOWLEDGMENTS

We'd like to express our appreciation to those people who helped in the creation of this book. Our thanks to Dick Roe, whose shepherding led us to this book. Chris gives thanks to his family, Bridget, Jasmine, and Jade, who inspire and sustain him in all that he does. Hadley would like to thank Lisa for letting him slip in the back door of Six Sigma, Scott for the first-rate instruction, and the NGST Six Sigma Black Belts and staff for all the good times.

Chapter One

Why Six Sigma?
Process Improvement Basics

Unlike lucky shoemakers, products do not just appear as the result of midnight visits from magic elves. The products and services delivered by any organization are the result of processes. Moreover, any process producing "on average" an acceptable product will be completely unacceptable to customers receiving one of many outputs that vary significantly from "the average." Customers are not comforted by the fact that the average product meets their needs when they experience the failure of an individual output. Processes are therefore improved when we can reduce the variation of the output produced and lower the total count of unsatisfied customers for all product deliveries, not just the average product delivery.

Six Sigma is a focused and disciplined approach to improving the quality of products and services by improving the processes by which they are produced. This chapter provides exercises to introduce the concepts of process, products, customer-defined quality, and the inherent process variations impeding customer satisfaction, in preparation for examining the Six Sigma tools and methodologies in more detail.

Section 1
What Is a Process?
Process Simulations

EXERCISE 1-1

Scrambled Letters (A Process Overview)

Description

Small teams compete to form words from random letters.

Purpose

- Recognize a basic process
- Identify input, process, and output variables
- Illustrate output variation

Time Required

30–40 minutes

- Exercise: 15–20 minutes
- Debrief: 15–20 minutes

Number of Participants

Two or more groups with 2 to 5 members (Equal group sizes are not required.)

Materials Required

- Letter tiles (Scrabble tiles work well) or paper slips
- Bag or container for letters
- Flip chart or overhead display

■ Watch or stopwatch (to time 20-second intervals)

■ Paper and pencil

Process

1. Divide participants into groups of 2 to 5 members.

2. Provide paper and pencils to each group.

3. Read or display the "Rules for Scrambled Words" below.

4. Place all the letters in the bag or container.

5. Draw 9 letters randomly from the bag or container.

6. Write the letters on a flip chart or overhead display.

7. Start the timer and let the teams make words for 20 seconds.

8. Count down the last 5 seconds and announce "pencils down."

9. Ask each group to report aloud their words and number of unused letters.

10. Record the number of unused letters for each group on the flip chart or overhead display.

11. Replace the letters into the bag or container.

12. Repeat the random draw and word-forming process 7 to 10 times.

13. Debrief the exercise.

Discussion Questions

■ What process did your group use to form words?

■ How did your process change from round to round?

- Why were the results different in each round of word forming?

- Why were group results different for the same letters?

- Were the variables related to your group process or the inputs to the process?

- What other game goals could we create and how would they impact the process?

Facilitator Notes

- The time per round can be increased to more than 20 seconds, but keep the time short enough to maintain time pressure and produce variation in the results.

- In the unlikely event of duplicate results in all rounds, go back and ask each team to disclose their words for the last few rounds and to use word differences to illustrate variation in output.

- When discussing the processes used by each group, generate a simple process map for one or more of the groups.

- Watch the groups as they develop their word list and note the differences during the discussion. Some groups develop a team process and work on a single list while other groups develop individual lists and pick the best result.

- When discussing the results, generate a list of variables and let the participants label each as part of the process or part of the input.

- Other game goals could be longest word, most words, or highest letter-value score.

- This exercise will be revisited and expanded upon in subsequent chapters.

Rules for Scrambled Words

1. Groups have 9 random letters.

2. Groups have 20 seconds to form words.

3. All words must be 3 or more letters.

4. Each of the 9 letters may be used only once.

5. Words may not be proper nouns or slang. (The decision of facilitator is final.)

6. Only a single list of words per team will be scored.

7. Game Goal: Fewest Unused Letters.

Example 1

Random Letters = P, B, F, S, R, E, S, A, M

Word List:

 MESS

 FAR

Result = 2 unused letters (P, B)

Example 2

Random Letters = D, G, O, P, R, E, T, A, T

Word List:

 DOG

 RAT

 PET

Result = 0 unused letters

Section 2
What Is a Product?
Value Propositions

EXERCISE 1-2
Group Bid (Customer Value)

Description

Participants bid on a $100 bill in an auction with a dynamic twist. This exciting game touches the most fundamental human emotion, greed.

Purpose

- Explore the dynamics of group decision making.

- Explore value propositions and how customer needs change over time.

Time Required

60 minutes

- Exercise: 30 minutes

- Debrief: 30 minutes

Materials

- Cash (A $100 bill gets attention, but a smaller amount can be used.)

- Paper and writing instruments

- Flip chart and markers

Number of Participants

Groups of 4 to 7, minimum of four groups

Process

1. Separate participants into small groups. Ask them to select a team name.

2. Show the cash to the participants and announce that one team will get the money.

3. Tell participants that they are customers at an auction and they have an opportunity to bid for the money. These are the rules for bidding:

   ■ Each team bids as a group, but they may split the cost of their bid and the prize money any way they wish.

   ■ Bids will be closed; each group will write its bid down and submit it.

   ■ Bidding will be done in rounds. The bidding will stop after the round when no new bids are received. Bids will be posted after each round.

   ■ Bids may not be reduced. Bids that are not increased carry over from round to round.

   ■ In each of the first 3 rounds the groups will have 3 minutes to submit their bid. No discussion between groups is permitted during the first 3 rounds.

   ■ After the third round, the following rounds (if necessary) will last 5 minutes and discussion between teams will be permitted.

   ■ When bidding is completed, the team that is the highest bidder pays what the members have bid and wins the money. (We usually accept only cash.)

- ■ The team that is the second highest bidder must pay what it bid also, but the members receive nothing.

- ■ Tell participants that their bids must have their team name and bid amount.

4. Answer any questions participants may have.

5. Tell them round 1 has begun and they have 3 minutes to submit their first bid.

6. At the end of each round collect bids and post them on flip chart. We usually create a matrix with the team names in the first column and bids for each team posted in successive columns (1 column per round).

7. At the end of each round, note which team is currently holding the winning bid and which team would be paying and receiving nothing.

8. When a round has passed in which no new bids are received, the bidding is complete.

9. Collect the money from the teams that had the first and second highest bids and award the money to the team with the highest bid.

10. Proceed to debrief.

Discussion Questions

Have the teams debrief in their small groups by answering the following questions. When complete, ask each team to share a key learning with the larger group.

- ■ How did your team frame the issue? (competition, sucker bet, easy money ...)

- ■ What process did your team use to make decisions? (consensus, majority rule, decision made by whoever was willing to put money on the line, etc.)

- As customers, what needs did you expect to be met by the auction process? How did your value proposition change as the rounds progressed?

- What needs were met or not met? As a customer, were you satisfied with this auction? Why or why not?

Facilitator Notes

- Make sure participants understand from the very beginning of the exercise that you will really take their money. If they don't believe this, the exercise loses its impact. One helpful tip is to announce that all proceeds will be donated to charity.

- Be prepared to make money. This exercise almost always brings in more than $100.

- If things get out of control and two teams are in a nonstop bidding war, stop the exercise and proceed to the debrief. The point of the exercise will have been made. In this case, you don't need to collect the money; but if you are donating the proceeds to charity, you can suggest a reasonable contribution.

EXERCISE 1-3

Vacation Planning (Exploring Value Propositions)

Description

Participants act as travel agents and customers planning a vacation to explore value propositions.

Purpose

- Demonstrate how value is derived from product attributes

- Demonstrate how broadly value is defined

- Demonstrate how customers perceive value differently
- Practice translating customer needs into product attributes and requirements

Time Required

60 minutes

Materials

Flip charts (1 for each group) and writing instruments

Number of Participants

This exercise is suited for groups of 6 to 10, but multiple groups can be run simultaneously.

Process

1. Separate participants into 2 groups: travel agents and customers who are planning a vacation.

2. Ask the travel agent group to create a vacation based on what members believe are the needs of their customers.

3. Ask the customer group to create a list of needs members want their vacation to fill.

4. Allow 10 minutes for groups to create their lists.

5. After 10 minutes, have the travel agent group present their vacation ideas to the customers. When they have finished, have the customers present their list of needs to the travel agents. (Allow approximately 10 minutes for both presentations.)

6. Have groups work together to compare the vacation attributes to the customer needs and jointly answer the following questions (20 minutes):

    - What are the attributes of the vacation?

- What are the differences between the needs met by the vacation attributes and the customer needs?

- What customer needs are not being met?

- Are there any "unspoken" customer needs (e.g., "safety")?

- What needs does the vacation meet that are not customer needs?

- How can the vacation be modified to meet all customer needs?

- How can you translate each customer need into a measurable product attribute? (For example, a customer need might be "a memorable experience"; the measure would be "tangible keepsakes included in the vacation package, like pictures and souvenirs.")

Discussion Questions

If you have multiple travel agents/customer groups, have them all debrief together (20 minutes).

- Were you able to design a single vacation that met all customer needs? Why or why not?

- Did some of the changes you made to the vacation to meet one need violate another?

- Should your Six Sigma projects try to satisfy all customer needs or most customer needs? Why?

Facilitator Notes

- If you have more than 10 participants, break them in to multiple groups of travel agents and customers.

- Physically separate the travel agent and customer groups so that they do not hear or see the work of the other group.

■ Participants may ask you if they should assume any financial constraints (i.e., are they planning a "dream" vacation or a "typical" vacation?). Do not answer this question directly; just reiterate the instructions to focus on needs.

Section 3
What Is a Quality Product?
Focusing on Customer Needs

EXERCISE 1-4

Custom Landscapes at Affordable Prices (Identifying the Process)

Description

Participants run a small business simulation, Custom Landscapes at Affordable Prices (CLAAP), producing customized works of art, and then they attempt to improve the process performance.

Purpose

■ Introduces the basic concepts of input, output, activity, customer, supplier, and quality metrics

■ Identify quality attributes

■ Provide participants an opportunity to discover and implement simple changes to demonstrate the relationships between process, products, and customer satisfaction

Time Required

60–90 minutes

■ Simulation 1: 20–30 minutes

- Debrief: 5–10 minutes

- Change Meeting: 15–20 minutes

- Simulation 2: 15–20 minutes

- Debrief: 5–10 minutes

Number of Participants
Groups of 8 to 10

Materials Required

- Job and customer descriptions, 1 per person
- Process simulation materials (per group)
  - Customer Order Forms (5)
  - CLAAP Pricing Sheet
  - Pens or pencils (4)
  - Box of crayons or colored felt pens
  - 12-inch ruler
  - Scissors (1 pair)
  - Construction paper, mixed colors (10 sheets)
  - Paper clips (3)
  - Glue stick or clear plastic tape
- Additional materials on hand for process change requests
  - Rulers
  - Scissors
  - Paper clips

- Glue sticks or clear plastic tape

- Blank name stickers or cardboard tents

Process

1. Review the CLAAP introduction with all the participants.

2. Divide participants into groups of 8 to 10 members; additional participants may watch the first simulation and then switch into customer roles for the second simulation.

3. Place each group at a table and provide 1 job description or customer description to each group member (Manager and Nurse are optional).

4. Provide each group with the process simulation materials. (*Note:* a prestocked shoe box for each group is convenient and reduces preparation time.)

5. After all participants have read their job instructions or customer description, start the simulation by asking the Bingo Parlor Manager to approach the Salesperson and submit an order.

6. Remind the participants they are running against the clock and delivery time is critical.

7. Thirty seconds after the Bingo Parlor Manager approaches the Salesperson, ask the Art Dealer to get in line to place an order with the Salesperson. Thirty seconds later, ask the Insurance Agent to get in line to place an order. Thirty seconds after that, ask the Nurse (if available) to get in line to place an order.

8. Let the simulation run until all orders are filled and surveys completed.

9. Debrief the first simulation with the questions below.

10. After the debrief tell all the groups they have 15 minutes to come up with no more than 2 changes to improve the CLAAP process. Customers should observe the meetings and be available to answer questions.

11. Restock the materials for each group during the change meeting.

12. At the end of the change meeting have each group announce their changes.

13. Run the simulation a second time with the new process changes in place.

14. Debrief the second simulation with the questions below.

Discussion Questions

- First Debrief

  - How do the customers feel about their purchase from CLAAP?

  - How can we tell if the CLAAP process is producing a quality product?

  - If we run the process again, how can we tell if we improved product quality and customer satisfaction?

- Second Debrief

  - What approaches or methods did your group use to identify problems and potential improvements?

  - How did your group decide which changes would be implemented?

  - What were the results of the process changes?

Facilitator Notes

■ Keep the process simulation moving by reminding the groups that delivery time is critical.

■ Focus the first simulation debriefing on the customer view of quality and the product output and not the solutions or potential fixes for the process.

■ Focus the second simulation debriefing on the process activities, improvement changes, and metrics.

■ With additional time the CLAAP simulation may be used to develop a project charter, Supplier, Input, Process, Output, Customer (SIPOC), and Critical to Quality (CTQ) tree.

■ This exercise will be revisited and expanded upon in subsequent chapters.

Custom Landscapes at Affordable Prices: Introduction

Custom Landscapes at Affordable Prices (CLAAP) produces scenic, low-cost works of art under a walk-up sales model. CLAAP subleases floor space for a sales desk and small production area inside a retail framing and art supply store. Customers place orders in person through a CLAAP salesperson and then wait or continue shopping until their custom piece is completed. Fast service and good value are the cornerstones of the CLAAP business model. Customer satisfaction is directly related to the amount of time the customer must wait for the landscape delivery. Previous customer interviews indicate dissatisfaction if wait time is more than a few minutes.

CLAAP owners are exploring the possibility of franchising the CLAAP concept. Having developed a standard Customer Order Form (COF) and job descriptions, the owners would like to evaluate the CLAAP process.

Your group will run the process for 3 or 4 customers, discuss the process, and then make no more than 2 improvements before running the process again.

CLAAP Job Description
Salesperson

The CLAAP Salesperson is the point of contact for CLAAP customers. The Salesperson takes customer orders and delivers completed landscapes to customers. The Salesperson uses the COF to record orders and initiate landscape production.

Job Instructions

- Greet each customer and fill in the COF by interviewing the customer.
- Give the completed COF to a Canvass Cutter.

- Upon receipt of a completed landscape:

  - Call out the customer name

  - Enter the time of order delivery on the COF

  - Calculate and enter the elapsed time from receipt to delivery on the COF

  - Detach the COF from the landscape

  - Hand the completed landscape to the customer

  - Complete the customer satisfaction survey with the customer

- At the end of each day clip together all COFs for delivered landscapes and give them to the Accountant for future billing.

Canvass Cutter

The CLAAP Canvass Cutter is responsible for cutting canvasses to custom sizes requested by the customer. The Canvass Cutter uses a ruler, pencil, and scissors to cut standard construction paper down to the size designated by each customer on the COF.

Job Instructions

- Upon receipt of a COF:

  - Pick a piece of standard construction paper

  - Read the COF to determine the required canvass size

  - Use the pencil and ruler to draw a rectangle of the required size on the construction paper

  - Use the scissors to cut out the rectangle

  - Attach the rectangle to the COF with a paper clip

- Deliver the COF and attached canvass to the Artist.

Artist

The CLAAP Artist is responsible for creating scenic landscapes on the precut canvasses. The Artist uses color sticks (crayons or pens) to add rolling hills, vegetation, animals, or structures to the canvass as designated on the COF.

Job Instructions

- Upon receipt of a COF and attached canvass:
    - Detach the COF from the canvass
    - Read the COF to determine the required basic features and custom options
    - Use the color sticks to draw the features and options on the canvass
    - Using a paper clip, attach the COF to the completed canvass
- Deliver the COF and attached canvass to the Framer.

Framer

The CLAAP Framer is responsible for adding a frame to the canvass landscape. The Framer uses standard construction paper, ruler, pencil, scissors, and tape to create framing strips, which attach to the canvass landscape to form a 1-inch border around the canvass.

Job Instructions

- Upon receipt of a COF and attached canvass:
    - Detach the COF from the canvass
    - Pick a piece of standard construction paper

- Cut 2 strips of paper 2 inches wide and 2 inches longer than the width of the canvass

- Cut 2 more strips of paper 2 inches wide and 2 inches longer than the height of the canvass

- Tape the 4 strips of paper to the back of the canvass to form a 1-inch border around the entire canvass

- Using a paper clip, attach the COF to the canvass

- Deliver the COF and attached landscape to the Accountant.

Accountant

The CLAAP Accountant is responsible for calculating the total price of each custom landscape and recording the price on the COF. After delivery of the landscape, the Accountant collects the COF for eventual use in the weekly billing process.

Job Instructions

- Upon receipt of a COF and attached canvass:

  - Calculate and enter the Basic Price in the Canvass Sizing section of the COF

  - Calculate and enter the Option Prices in the Custom Features section of the COF

  - Add the Option Prices to the Basic Price and enter the Total Price on the COF

- Deliver the COF and attached landscape to the Salesperson.

Manager (Optional)

The CLAAP Manager is responsible for the overall operation of the business. The Manager drinks coffee and keeps a watchful eye on the other employees.

Job Instructions

- Be helpful and supportive without performing any of the functions of the other employees.
- Schmooze with customers and suppliers.

CLAAP Customer Description

Bingo Parlor Manager

As manager of the Big Bucks Bingo Parlor you use the CLAAP landscapes as door prizes for your nightly events. Appearance and inexpensive price are important factors, but your biggest concerns are the superstitions of your bingo patrons. Money-green and heavenly-blue appear to be highly prized by your gray-haired gamblers while black, brown, and red send stamp crazy players stomping out the door. Looking for any edge, the ink-fingered regulars have come to believe the landscape door prizes represent a financial barometer of their nightly fate. You are always on the lookout for supernatural implications, real or imagined, in the CLAAP landscapes.

Art Dealer

As an art dealer working within the cutting-edge Post Quality movement you unearth the works of unknown artists, buy at bargain prices, and resell at huge markups to wealthy entertainers, athletes, and leaders of foreign nations. You prize uniqueness and unconventional artistic merit. Controversial pieces with an unintelligible and incoherent message are highly desired. Although most respected art critics have labeled the Post Quality movement as a fly-by-night con game , you and your associates are passionate about both the art and the cash flow.

Insurance Agent

As an insurance agent traveling throughout the country, your sales and resulting commissions are directly tied to the number of potential clients you can contact each day. Your supervisor has asked you to take time out of your busy working day to pick up a CLAAP landscape for the outer reception area of the home office. You are not happy about this request. Your only goals are to get the landscape as quickly as possible and make sure the landscape is sturdy enough to survive the overhead compartment on the plane ride home. Your art-loving boss has also requested a receipt for the company-required expense report.

Nurse (Optional)

As a nurse in a mobile vaccination center for school children, you use the CLAAP landscapes as cheerful wall decorations. On occasion the landscapes serve as a helpful distraction for the most apprehensive children. Value and child-friendly appearance are your primary motivations for purchasing CLAAP landscapes.

CLAPP Customer Order Form

Customer Information

Name _____

Billing Address _____

Process Time Information

Time of Order Receipt _____

Time of Order Delivery _____

Elapsed Time (from receipt to delivery) _____

Canvass Sizing

Height (from 3 to 8 inches) _____   Basic Price

Width (from 3 to 11 inches) _____   Height × Width × $0.20 = $_____

Custom Features

			Unit Price	Option Prices
Land:	☐ Hills	☐ Plains	☐ Beach $ _____	$ _____
Sky:	☐ Sunny	☐ Cloudy	☐ Snowy $ _____	$ _____
Structures:	☐ Barn	☐ House	☐ Fence $ _____	$ _____

Trees: Count _____   @ $0.20 ea. = $ _____

Bushes: Count _____   @ $0.20 ea. = $ _____

Animals: Type _____   Count _____   @ $0.50 ea. = $ _____

            Type _____   Count _____   @ $0.50 ea. = $ _____

            Type _____   Count _____   @ $0.50 ea. = $ _____

Total Price (Basic Plus Options) $_____

CLAPP Customer Satisfaction Survey

1. CLAAP service is fast, friendly, and helpful.
☐ Strongly Agree ☐ Agree ☐ Disagree ☐ Strongly Disagree ☐ Not Sure

2. CLAAP landscapes are attractive and desirable pieces of art.
☐ Strongly Agree ☐ Agree ☐ Disagree ☐ Strongly Disagree ☐ Not Sure

3. CLAAP landscapes are a good value.
☐ Strongly Agree ☐ Agree ☐ Disagree ☐ Strongly Disagree ☐ Not Sure

---

CLAAP Pricing Sheet

Description	Price
Basic Landscape (Includes choice of land, sky, and structure)	$0.20 per square inch
Trees (Optional)	$0.20 each
Bushes (Optional)	$0.20 each
Animals (Optional)	$0.50 each

Section 4
Why Is Each Product Slightly Different?
Demonstrating Process Variation

EXERCISE 1-5
Eyedropper (Examining Process Variation)

Description

Participants use an eyedropper to examine process variation in an everyday context.

Purpose

- Demonstrate how process variation exists in even the most simple of processes.

- Help participants identify and recognize the many sources of process variation.

Time Required

45 minutes

Materials

- 1 eyedropper per group, preferably with little or no markings on it
- 1 cup of water per group
- Paper and writing instruments for record keeping

Number of Participants

Groups of 3 or 4

Process

1. Ask each group to identify a record keeper and a process implementer. Remaining group members will be process observers.

2. Perform the process:

   - Have each process implementer place the eyedropper in the cup of water, squeeze the bulb, and draw the eyedropper out.

   - Ask them to expel the water from the eyedropper back into the cup 1 drop at a time.

   - Instruct the process observers to count the number of drops.

   - Ask the recorder to write down the number of drops.

3. Repeat the process (step 2).

4. Repeat the process again (step 2).

5. Perform the first debrief below.

6. Ask groups to repeat the experiment, but to take steps to minimize variation in the results.

7. Have each group select a new process implementer and then repeat the experiment.

Discussion Questions

■ First Debrief

■ What are the sources of variation in the number of drops?

■ Which sources of variation are controllable by the groups? Uncontrollable? Why?

■ Second Debrief

■ How did a new process implementer impact the results? Why?

■ What does variation in a simple process tell us about variation in a more complex process?

Facilitator Notes

■ Use both the variation within the group and the variation between groups as points of discussion.

■ Most groups will mark the eyedropper to reduce variation in the results.

■ Sources of in-process variation include how hard the bulb is squeezed when withdrawing water, how the bulb is squeezed when expelling water, changes in the condition of the eyedropper as it's being used, etc.

■ Point out that input variation would be increased if each team worked with a different fluid (water, oil, milk, etc.)

■ Other possible sources of variation include accuracy of the counting by the process observers (measurement variation).

Chapter Two

Who's on First?
Roles and Organization

Six Sigma encompasses more than just process improvement tools and methodologies. Improvement results from people and their ability to manage change effectively and therefore relies heavily on the organizational infrastructure put in place to support the initiative. Organizational roles must be well defined and clearly communicated for successful change management. Six Sigma involves leaders, facilitators, mentors, stakeholders, process owners, and, too often, critics and bystanders. This chapter provides games that will help participants define roles and perform them well.

Section 1
Team Roles

EXERCISE 2-1
Give–Get (Six Sigma Roles and Expectations)

Description

Using the matrix worksheet that is provided below, participants define required contributions and expected benefits for specific job functions across a variety of roles within the Six Sigma initiative.

Purpose

- Provide an overview of Six Sigma roles and organization.

- Define expectations for both the overall initiative and the performance of individual projects.

Time Required

30–40 minutes

- Exercise: 20–25 minutes

- Debrief: 10–15 minutes

Number of Participants

Any number; groups of 3 to 5 work well

Materials Required

Give–Get Worksheet

Process

1. Provide each participant with a Give–Get Worksheet.

2. Instruct participants to enter for each job function (row) both the expected contribution ("gives") to the activities (columns) and return benefit ("gets") from the activities.

3. Instruct the participants to complete the worksheet with as many items as possible.

4. Debrief the exercise.

Discussion Questions

■ For which, if any, of the job functions are the contributions and benefits unclear or not defined? What could be done to better define the expectations?

■ Are there any job functions that are significantly unbalanced between contributions and benefits? What could be done to improve the balance?

Facilitator Notes

■ Remind participants to move quickly through the boxes and not to dwell on any box too long; complete as many boxes as possible.

■ Tailor the job functions to the specific organization or Six Sigma initiative, or alternatively have the participants prepare a list of job functions or stakeholders.

■ This exercise is ideally performed by participants after an introduction to the Six Sigma initiative and organization.

Give–Get Worksheet

Instructions: For each job function (row) enter both the expected contribution ("gives") to the activities (columns) and return benefit ("gets") from the activities.

	Project Performance	*Facilitation/ Mentorship*	*Process Implementation*	*Leadership/ Oversight*
Process Owners				
Sponsors/ Champions				
Project Team Members				
Team Leads				
Black Belts				
Management Council				
Process Users				
Customers				
Suppliers				

EXERCISE 2-2

Lights, Camera, Action (Dealing with Difficult Situations)

Description

An improvisational role-playing exercise demonstrating difficult situations faced by various roles within the Six Sigma initiative.

Purpose

- Identify potentially difficult situations encountered by various roles within a Six Sigma initiative.

- Identify expectations and goals for the different roles within a Six Sigma initiative.

- Share effective and ineffective methods for dealing with difficult situations encountered by various roles.

Time Required

45–60 minutes (3–4 scenes)

- Setup: Done in advance of meeting
- Exercise: 5 minutes per scene
- Debrief: 5–10 minutes per scene

Number of Participants

12 or more

Materials Required

Index Cards

Advance Setup

Ask participants or groups of participants to develop and submit a set of Interaction and Player cards (as described below) for a single difficult situation typically faced by any of the roles within a Six Sigma initiative.

Interaction Card

Players: Identify 2 or more roles (Black Belt, Process Owner, Instructor, Champion, Project Team Member, Student, etc.)

Setting: Where does the interaction take place? (In a conference room, office, elevator, classroom, etc.)

Purpose: Why have the players come together? (For a staff meeting, process mapping, training, etc.)

Opening Dialogue: First statement for 1 or more of the players. (Identify player(s) and provide quote(s)).

Player Objective Cards

Provide a separate card to each player describing the point of conflict and that player's objective for the interaction. Describe any other pertinent information regarding motives, goals, private agendas, biases, history, etc.

Process

1. Read the Interaction Card to the entire audience.

2. Select a volunteer for each role.

3. Provide the appropriate Player Objective Card to each volunteer.

4. While the players review their roles, arrange the scene with any available props (tables, chairs, flip charts, etc.).

5. Have players start with the predetermined dialogue and allow them to "improvise" for a few more minutes. The total scene should run 5 minutes or less.

6. Hold a group discussion with both the players and the audience.

Discussion Questions

- What is the inherent conflict or difficulty?

- What were the objectives of each player?

- What are the expectations of the organization for each of the Six Sigma roles?

- What techniques are effective or ineffective in these situations?

Facilitator Notes

- For a fun twist to this exercise have players pick a famous actor, historical figure, or popular movie/TV character in which they will perform their role.

- Facilitators may optionally create the card sets in advance with the assistance of the session leaders or sponsors.

- Read through the submissions in advance and pick a good cross section of roles and issues for the audience.

Section 2
Leadership

EXERCISE 2-3
Team Poker (Leadership and Decision Making)

Description

Participants work in small teams to try to create 5 "pat" poker hands from 25 randomly selected playing cards.

Purpose

- Illustrate the dynamics of how leadership emerges on unstructured teams

- Demonstrate the impacts of leadership on team performance

- Explore decision-making alternatives

Time Required

- Exercise: 20 minutes
- Debrief: 20 minutes

Number of Participants

Teams of 3 to 7 (This can be run with just 1 team, but multiple teams create a competitive atmosphere that energizes the exercise.)

Materials Required

Playing Cards (1 deck for each team)

Process

1. Divide participants into teams of 3 to7 people.

2. Explain the objectives and procedures to participants:

   ■ Each team will deal themselves 25 cards from a randomly shuffled deck.

   ■ The team objective is to create 5 "pat" hands from their 25 cards as fast as possible.

   ■ A "pat" hand consists of 5 cards that make a flush (all the same suit), straight (unbroken sequence), full-house (three of a kind plus a pair), or one containing four of a kind.

   ■ There are 2 phases: planning (10 minutes) and implementation (10 minutes).

   ■ Teams may exchange cards for a new, randomly dealt card with a penalty of 15 seconds for each exchanged card.

   ■ Teams should inform the facilitator when they have met their objective. Optionally you may offer a prize for the team that completes the exercise in the shortest, penalty-adjusted time.

3. Start the planning phase. The teams may play with the cards during this time.

4. At the end of 10 minutes, ask teams to shuffle their cards and deal themselves 25 cards.

5. Start the implementation phase.

Discussion Questions

   ■ Did the team have an effective plan?

   ■ Did the team make good use of all of its resources (was everyone involved)?

   ■ How were decisions made?

- How did time pressure impact the team's decision making and effectiveness?

- How was leadership of the group handled? How did leadership impact performance?

Facilitator Notes

- Five "pat" hands can almost always be made from 25 randomly selected cards and exchanging cards is almost never necessary.

- An individual familiar with the task can complete this task in less than 2 minutes and most teams can complete the task in less than the 10 minutes allowed.

EXERCISE 2-4

Historical Leaders (Urgency, Vision, and Message)

Description

Participants are asked to fill in the blanks for historical examples of leadership and are then asked to identify the communicated agenda of current leaders.

Purpose

- Demonstrate the significance and effectiveness of urgency, vision, and message for mobilizing change in large organizations or populations

- Identify the urgency, vision, and message of the current organization

Time Required

10–20 minutes

- Exercise: 5–10 minutes
- Debrief: 5–10 minutes

Number of Participants

Groups of 3 to 5

Materials Required

- Historical Leaders handout that follows
- Current Leaders handout that follows

Process

1. Split participants into groups of 3 to 5.

2. Provide the handout of Historical and Current Leaders to each participant.

3. Instruct the groups to first discuss and fill in the missing information for each line of the Historical Leaders handout.

4. Instruct the groups to identify urgency, mission, and message for currently recognized social, political, or business leaders.

5. Debrief the exercise when all groups have completed the task.

Discussion Questions

- How do sense of urgency, vision, and message impact motivation?
- How are sense of urgency, vision, and message used most effectively by leaders?
- What are the urgencies, vision, and message of your organization as expressed by current leadership?

Facilitator Notes

- Remind participants that leadership effectiveness is illustrated here solely by an ability to motivate large groups and is not based on the direction of the leadership, which may be good or evil.

- Missing information for historical leaders table:

  Line 1 = Cold War, "...bring down the wall."

  Line 2 = Space/Technology Preeminence, JFK

  Line 3 = Racial Discrimination, "I have a dream..."

  Line 4 = Master Race, Hitler

- Discussion of leadership effectiveness can include identification of audience and constituents, clarity of communication, as well as linkage of message, vision, and urgency.

Historical Leaders

Sense of Urgency (Event/Threat)	Vision	Message (Mission)	Leader
???	One Super Power	???	Ronald Reagan
Russian Space Program	???	Walk on moon before end of decade	???
???	Equality	???	Martin Luther King
Germany's Great Depression	???	Ethnic cleansing	???

Current Leaders

Sense of Urgency (Event/Threat)	Vision	Message (Mission)	Leader

Section 3
Facilitation and Mentoring

EXERCISE 2-5
Meeting Facilitation (Role Play)

Description

Participants observe a role play where 1 participant facilitates a meeting with some difficult attendees.

Purpose

- Demonstrate the role of the facilitator in running an effective meeting
- Provide examples of some challenges facilitators face
- Explore effective and ineffective facilitation techniques

Time Required

40 minutes

Materials Required

- Flip Chart and pens
- Observer sheets (see below)
- Role descriptions (see below)

Number of Participants

Seven role players with unlimited observers

Process

1. Select 1 volunteer to play the role of facilitator.

2. Select 6 more volunteers to play other meeting roles.

3. Arrange the role players in a circle that is easily observed by remaining participants.

4. Announce to all participants that the volunteers are having a meeting. Say: "The goal of this meeting is to identify the 5 biggest risks or obstacles to a successful Six Sigma project. The meeting is scheduled for 20 minutes."

5. Read the facilitator's role description aloud and hand it to the facilitator.

6. Hand out the role descriptions to the other role players.

7. Ask them to read their descriptions to themselves.

8. Hand out Observer Sheets to remaining participants.

9. Ask the facilitator to start the meeting when that person is ready.

10. End the meeting after 20 minutes has passed or when the facilitator declares the meeting complete.

11. Ask role players to read aloud their role description.

Discussion Questions

- Ask the facilitator to describe how he or she felt during the meeting. What did the person find particularly challenging?

- Ask the observers to share their observations. What facilitation techniques were particularly effective?

- How might the facilitator have handled something differently?

Facilitator Notes

- Provide role players with their own role description only. Do not allow them to see the roles others are playing.

- You'll need 2 copies of the Feuding Rivals role. When handing these out, let each person know who his or her rival is.

- In general, do not interfere with the meeting.

- Make sure to praise the person who volunteers to be the facilitator for that person's courage and willingness to help the rest of the participants learn.

- During the debrief guide observations of the facilitation techniques to learning points. Don't let it become a session of criticizing the facilitator.

Meeting Facilitation Role Descriptions

Facilitator Your role is to perform the following facilitation responsibilities and guide the meeting to a successful outcome:

- Listener

- Clarifier

- Gatekeeper

- Summarizer

- Shepherd

- Timekeeper

- Consensus Tester

Dominator Your role is to participate very actively during this session. Share any ideas you may have no matter how good or bad you think they may be. You assume that the other people in the meeting don't know as much about this topic as you do so their ideas don't deserve as much consideration as yours do.

Naysayer You are a highly critical thinker. Look for what might be wrong with any ideas presented and voice your concerns.

Reluctant You have ideas to contribute but are reluctant to express them. Speak only if you are asked to do so.

Digressor You really don't care much about this topic and would like to talk about something else. Try to segue the comments of others to a totally different topic.

Feuding Rivals (2 volunteers) You really don't like the person you are feuding with and believe that person's ideas are not worthy of merit. Feel free to voice your concerns, as you know that person doesn't like you either. Exhibit as much hostility as is likely to be exhibited in your organization's culture.

Meeting Facilitation Role-Play Observers Sheet

Participants in this meeting are playing the following roles:

- Dominator

- Naysayer

- Reluctant

- Digressor

- Feuding Rivals

What did the facilitator do to handle each of these roles? Were the facilitator's actions effective or ineffective?

_____

_____

_____

_____

_____

Look for how the facilitator performs the following responsibilities:

- Listener

- Clarifier

- Gatekeeper

- Summarizer

- Shepherd

- Timekeeper

- Consensus Tester

EXERCISE 2-6

10 Things I Do for Fun (Team Icebreaker)

Description

Participants interact and build relationships around the things they do for fun.

Purpose

- Provide participants with an "icebreaker" they can use with their project teams

- Break down barriers to open communication

- Allow team members to see each other in a context different than work

- Build camaraderie among team members

Time Required

15–30 minutes depending on the number of participants

Materials

Paper and writing instruments

Number of Participants

This exercise is suited for groups of 5 to 50.

Process

1. Share the name of the activity and its objectives.

2. Ask each participant to write down 10 things they currently do for fun. Give them about 5 minutes to complete this. Many people struggle to list more than a few items.

3. When participants have completed their lists (some will not have 10 and that's OK), ask them to mingle and find the person in the room who has the most activities in common with them.

Discussion Questions

Debriefing is optional, but for many working professionals this exercise can highlight the lack of balance between fun and work.

- How hard was it to think of 10 things you do for fun?

- Did you find it surprisingly hard or easy?

- Do you want to spend more or less time having fun?

Facilitator Notes

- Remind participants they are to list activities they *currently* do, not things they have done in the past.

- If participants are really struggling to list activities, you can suggest things like reading, tennis, golf, watching sports, playing with children, etc.

- Avoid making this a competition. If participants see this as a competition they will hurriedly move from person to person without building relationships. Encourage them to take their time when comparing activities.

Chapter Three

What Is Our Quest?
The Define Phase

A critical first step, the Define Phase plots the course for successful process improvement. In the Define Phase we (1) state the observed problem, (2) identify a business case for addressing the problem, (3) establish scope and boundaries for the project, and (4) determine the critical measures of customer satisfaction.

As is often repeated but rarely followed, "A problem well stated is a problem half solved." Too many projects of every type head off with the best intention of righting all wrongs but ultimately flounder in misunderstanding and frustration. Without effective problem and goal statements, "declared victory" is the frequently recognized, yet hardly beneficial exit strategy. A clear, concise, objective problem statement with a quantifiable goal is the first step toward a meaningful contribution to the business.

Benefits to the business are the underlying reason for improvement projects. Committing the necessary time and resources to improvement projects are only justified by an expected return of benefits to the business: Business benefits could be cost reduction, profit or sales increase, improved cash flow, higher asset utilization, or any other benefit that may be weighed against the required investment. Whether precisely calculated or intuitively estimated, the business case must serve as the rationale for starting a project and continuing through each phase of Define, Measure, Analyze, Improve, and Control (DMAIC).

Establishing project boundaries will increase focus and prevent overload. The temptation to charter projects with a wide or unlimited project scope can be debilitating to team performance and project success. Team morale and positive results rely on a narrowing of the project charter to actionable problems in a single area of clearly defined process ownership.

Identifying a problem implies that we need to make the product better. But first we need to know what "better" really means. To coin a phrase, "Better is in the eye of the beholder." The "beholder" of a product or service is the customer. Unfortunately customers and their needs can be complex and difficult to interpret. Even when asked directly, many customers don't express in simple, measurable terms their desired attributes for the product or service. Six Sigma projects must translate the often vague and ambiguous needs of customers into clearly defined, measurable attributes with an acceptable or not acceptable level of performance called *a specification.* The resulting attributes are called *critical to quality* (CTQ). Each unacceptable performance of a CTQ is known as a *defect.* Together, CTQs, specifications, and defects are the measurement basis for determining "better" on a Six Sigma project.

The exercises in this chapter will help participants sharpen their ability to define meaningful, solvable, properly scoped projects with importance to the business and a focus on critical customer needs.

Section 1
What Hurts?
Formulating Problem and Goal Statements

EXERCISE 3-1
Doctor, Doctor (Stating the Problem and Goal)

Description

Participants listen to a series of dialogues between a doctor and patient in order to develop problem and goal statements.

Purpose

- Practice generating and testing problem and goal statements
- Identify common pitfalls for the development of problem and goal statements
- Understand the ultimate impact of problem and goal statements on project performance

Time Required

20–30 minutes

- Exercise: 10–15 minutes
- Debrief: 10–15 minutes

Number of Participants

Two or more groups of 3 to 5

Materials Required

- Problem Statement Worksheet (see below)

- Doctor/Patient Dialogue Sheets (see below)

Process

1. Split into groups of 3 to 5 people.

2. Provide a Problem and Goal Statement Worksheet and Dialogue Sheet to each group.

3. Instruct the groups to develop a problem and goal statement by using the worksheet after each of the three dialogues.

4. Allow 3 to 5 minutes per dialogue.

Discussion Questions

- What was your final problem and goal statement? How would differences in these statements impact the future actions of the doctor, patient, or patient's wife?

- What are the pitfalls and difficulties of developing a good problem and goal statement? What natural human tendencies conflict with developing a good problem and goal statement?

- How would a well-written or poorly written problem and goal statement impact the improvement project? How could a problem and goal statement impact the relationship between the team and process owner?

- What are some effective techniques and methodologies for drawing out meaningful problem and goal statements?

Facilitator Notes

- There may be some confusion after the first dialogue. Encourage participants to record something in the worksheet but offer no additional information or suggestions.

- Encourage participants to be good time managers and complete all 3 dialogues in the time allowed.

- Problem statements and goals may be developed for either the husband or the wife; explore both in the discussion.

- On an overhead or flipchart, record the exact words generated by different teams when discussing the final results. There are often subtle differences in wording, which could have a large impact on the future actions of the doctor, husband, or wife.

- During the discussion participants may recall experiences with poor problem and goal statements. Try to solicit examples of good problem and goal statements, which may then be compared in format, development, and results to the examples of poor statements.

- Review the sample problem and goal statement worksheet provided below prior to facilitating this exercise.

Doctor/Patient Dialogues

Dialogue 1

DOCTOR: What seems to be the problem?

PATIENT: My wife told me I should see a doctor, so I made this appointment. If I don't see a doctor, she's going to leave me and go home to her mother.

Dialogue 2

DOCTOR: Why would your wife want to leave you and go home to her mother?

PATIENT: She doesn't want to go home to her mother, but for the last three weeks she has been irritable and cranky every morning. When I told her she was cranky she threw a broken alarm clock at my head.

Dialogue 3

DOCTOR: Why would your wife behave that way?

PATIENT: I don't think she is getting enough sleep. She told me I snore so loud I shook the alarm clock off the nightstand. I guess the poor old gal just can't sleep without the nice soothing tick of the alarm clock.

Problem and Goal Statement Sample Worksheet

	Dialogue 1	Dialogue 2	Dialogue 3
What is the general area of concern or opportunity?			
What are the observed effects and conditions (good and bad)?			
What are the consequences of not addressing the concern or opportunity?			
Write a simple statement of the observed problem (symptom and effect) using a noun–verb format. State a measurable goal for improvement.			
What, if any, opinions or judgments are included in the problem statement?			

Problem and Goal Statement Sample Worksheet (*Continued*)

	Dialogue 1	Dialogue 2	Dialogue 3
What, if any, presumed causes are included in the problem statement?			
Who or what is assigned blame, if any, by the problem statement?			
Identify any presumed solutions in the problem statement.			
Are there multiple problems included in the problem statement?			
Rewrite the problem statement without opinions, judgments, blame, presumed causes, solutions, or compound problems.			

Problem and Goal Statement Sample Worksheet

	Dialogue 1	*Dialogue 2*	*Dialogue 3*
What is the general area of concern or opportunity?	Husband's well-being	Husband's well-being	Wife's well-being
What are the observed effects and conditions (good and bad)?	Husband's appointment Husband at doctor's office	Three weeks of morning irritability One incident of violent behavior	Three weeks of morning irritability One incident of violent behavior
What are the consequences of not addressing the concern or opportunity?	Wife departure Husband suffers	Continued irritability of wife Annoyance to husband Physical harm to husband	Lack of sleep for wife Irritability of wife Annoyance to husband Physical harm to husband
Write a simple statement of the observed problem (symptom and effect) using a noun–verb format. State a measurable goal for improvement.	Husband's refusal to see a doctor exposes wife to illness. Goal is to keep wife healthy and home with husband.	Wife's morning disposition has declined over the last three weeks. Goal is elimination of irritability.	Wife losing sleep when husband snores resulting in irritability. Goal is no snoring.
What, if any, opinions or judgments are included in the problem statement?	Illness of husband Exposure of wife to illness	Wife is irritable	None

Problem and Goal Statement Sample Worksheet (*Continued*)

	Dialogue 1	Dialogue 2	Dialogue 3
What, if any, presumed causes are included in the problem statement?	Refusal to see a doctor	None	Snoring causes wife to lose sleep.
Who or what is assigned blame, if any, by the problem statement?	Husband is to blame.	None	None
Identify any presumed solutions in the problem statement.	Seeing a doctor will eliminate the problem.	None	None
Are there multiple problems included in the problem statement?	None	None	None
Rewrite the problem statement without opinions, judgments, blame, presumed causes, solutions, or compound problems.	Husband losing wife. Goal is to keep husband and wife together.	Husband experiencing irritable wife over the last three weeks. Goal is reduced reports of wife irritability and thrown objects.	Wife losing sleep when husband snores. Goal is no loss of sleep.

Section 2
Why Do We Need to "Get Better"?
Stating the Business Case for Change

EXERCISE 3-2

Precision Delivery Inc. (Stating the Business Case for Improvement)

Description

This exercise is a team competition to create approved project problem statements and business cases for Precision Delivery Inc., a package pickup and delivery service company. The Precision Delivery Inc. (PDI) case will be revisited in subsequent chapters and may be followed through each phase of the DMAIC process.

Purpose

- Practice generating, quantifying, and testing problem statements and business cases

- Identify potential criteria for project selection

- Understand the ultimate impact of the business case on project performance

Time Required

40–60 minutes

- Exercise: 30–40 minutes

- Debrief: 10–20 minutes

Number of Participants

Two or more groups of 4 to 6

Materials Required

- Precision Delivery Inc. Case Study (see below)
- Project Proposal Worksheet (see below)

Process

1. Split into Project Development Teams of 4 to 6 people.

2. Select 1 person from each group to serve on the Executive Project Approval Board (EPAB).

3. Distribute the Precision Delivery Inc. Case Study and the PDI Project Proposal Worksheet to the EPAB members.

4. Send the EPAB members to a corner or out of the room and give them 20 minutes to read the case, review the proposal worksheet, and develop a set of guidelines for project approval.

5. Distribute the PDI case study and project proposal worksheets to the Project Development Teams.

6. Inform the Project Development Teams that they will have 30 minutes to prepare project proposals and that the EPAB approval guidelines will be available in roughly 20 minutes. Each Project Development Team may submit no more than 4 proposals. The winning team will be determined by the highest total benefits for approved projects (not number of approved projects).

7. After 20 minutes have the EPAB read aloud (or distribute) the project approval guidelines without allowing questions from the Project Development Teams. Announce that all proposals will be due in 10 minutes.

8. Instruct the EPAB members to spend the next 10 minutes discussing their approach for validating benefit amounts on the project proposal worksheets

9. At the end of 30 minutes collect the worksheets and distribute them randomly to each of the EPAB members for rejection/approval and benefit validation.

10. Tell the EPAB members they have 10 minutes to assign a benefit amount to all approved proposals and post the team scores.

11. Begin the debriefing discussion with the Project Development Teams while the EPAB members tally the results.

Discussion Questions

■ Were the projects easy or difficult to identify? Why?

■ How did you quantify the benefits?

■ How did you deal with missing information?

■ How many potential proposals did you identify and how did you decide which proposals to submit?

■ What are the potential interactions between projects?

■ How did the EPAB generate approval guidelines and validate the benefits? What worked and what didn't work?

■ How does the project selection process impact an organization's Six Sigma initiative?

■ Where would project proposals be developed in your organization?

Facilitator Notes

- Participants typically want additional information and more time but keep the clock running and address the shortcomings of suboptimal information and time in the debrief.

- Interactions between projects are sometimes difficult to extract but make sure potential relationships are identified (e.g., projects reducing rebates may interact, even conflict, with projects reducing idle time).

- The discussion should progress from PDI specific issues to more general observations pertaining to your organization.

- This exercise will be revisited and expanded upon in subsequent chapters.

PDI Project Proposal Worksheet

Team Name: _____

Project Title: _____

Problem Statement: _____

_____

_____

Goal Statement: _____

Business Case and Estimated Benefits: _____

_____

_____

Benefit Calculations or Basis: _____

_____

_____

Executive Project Approval Board Use Only

Approval: Yes?   No?

Verified Benefits Amount: ☐   ☐

Directions for Completing the Project Proposal Worksheet

Team Name: To be chosen by the Project Development Team. Enter the team name on all project proposals.

Project Title: Identified for the project. Should reflect the goal of the project (Decrease Widget Rework, Reduce Billing Cycle Time, Improve Product Line Cash Flow, etc.)

Problem Statement: Observed conditions and impact on business (e.g., 20% of widgets reworked resulting in added cost of $6.50 per unit)

Goal Statement: Quantitative goal for improvement project (e.g., Reduce widget rework to less than 5%)

Business Case and Estimated Benefits: Describe the business benefit and the estimated impact (e.g., Decreasing widget product cost increases product margin resulting in $1.2M additional profit before tax per year)

Benefit Calculations or Basis: Provide justification or rationale for the business case and estimated benefits (e.g., 100,000 widgets per month produced $\times$ 15% reworked units eliminated $6.50/widget for rework $\times$ 12 months = $1.2M Annual Profit Before Tax)

EPAB Approval: See published guidelines

EPAB Verified Benefits Amount: EPAB adjusted estimate of benefits

Precision Delivery Inc. Case Study

Precision Delivery Inc. (PDI) is a package pickup and delivery service for homes and small businesses. PDI specializes in packages 50 pounds or less and has a full-price rebate policy for any pickup or delivery made outside the customer-designated 15-minute window. PDI advertising proudly states, "Pickup and delivery at your convenience, not ours."

PDI has facilities at 2 locations, Downtown and Suburbia, each servicing customers within a 15-mile radius with pickup and deliveries made by truck or bicycle. Customers designate a 15-minute window for their packages to be picked up or delivered. PDI charges customers $5 per package plus $1 per pound (50-pound maximum).

PDI Sales Operators receive pickup and delivery requests by phone from customers. Dispatchers issue instructions to Field Operators for pickups and deliveries. To ensure prompt service, Dispatchers plan for 30 minutes of travel time, one way, for each pickup or delivery and target arrival time for the start of the 15-minute window. Under current procedures, travel time in excess of 45 minutes will result in a rebate and travel time less than 30 minutes results in idle time for the Field Operator. Field Operators return directly to the dispatch facility after each pickup or delivery.

A subcontractor who offers bike and truck time on demand supplies Field Operations. PDI pays only for round-trip road time and idle time at the customer destination. PDI accountants have calculated the Field Operations variable cost for delivery, pickup, and idle time at $7.50/hour for bicycles and $15.00/hour for trucks. All other costs are fixed at $5,000 per week. Pickups and deliveries are made Monday through Friday, 8:00 a.m. to 4:00 p.m.

Recently, Sales Operators have reported a noticeable increase in customer concern for the timeliness of deliveries and pickup. In response, Sales Operators were instructed to remind customers of the PDI price rebate policy. Additionally, a short survey was sent out to a small group of established customers. Survey results disclosed an appreciation of price rebates, but a preference for deliveries within the promised 15-minute window.

PDI's CEO and sole shareholder, Pat Hunter, is concerned about customer satisfaction and profitability. Although financial results have been consistent over the last year, Pat believes the current return on sales (ROS) of 11% must increase to more than 20% to avoid shutting down the business and more than 30% to grow the business. Pat wants to know how PDI can increase ROS while maintaining or increasing customer satisfaction.

Last month, PDI had the following results:

Sales	$58,500
Sales after Rebates	$49,100
Field Operations Trip Cost (Variable)	$18,900
Field Operations Idle Time Cost (Variable)	$ 3,600
Gross Margin	$26,600
General and Administrative (Fixed)	$20,000
Profit Before Tax	$ 6,600

Section 3
Where Will We Improve?
Determining Project Scope

EXERCISE 3-3
Break it Down (Individual Process Map)

Description

A Supplier, Input, Process, Output, Customer (SIPOC) exercise where individuals map a process and then receive feedback from another person on the clarity of their process boundaries and scope.

Purpose

- Teach participants to define and articulate a basic process description

- Illustrate a simple technique for identifying process scope

- Demonstrates the dynamics of communicating process scope to another person

Time Required

45 minutes

- 10 minutes for setup and completion of worksheet

- 20 minutes for clarification coaching session

- 15 minutes for debrief

Number of Participants

Participants work in pairs.

Materials Required

SIPOC Worksheet (see below)

Process

1. Ask participants to think of a process with which they are familiar and proficient.

2. Introduce the SIPOC Worksheet. Explain that the participants are to list the inputs and outputs to the task/process and the steps required to complete the task/process.

3. Allow 5 minutes for participants to complete the worksheet. Provide a time update when 1 minute is remaining.

4. Have each participant select a partner to work with. Instruct participants to take turns reviewing their partner's SIPOC Worksheet and exploring the following issues:

    ■ Did the worksheet clearly define start and end events?

    ■ Is the worksheet clear enough to create a common understanding of the basic process and scope?

5. Allow 20 minutes for the discussion. Halfway into the time allotted, remind participants to be good time managers and allow each person the opportunity for feedback.

Discussion Questions

■ Was it easy or difficult to identify the inputs, outputs, and process steps of a task/process you are familiar with?

■ How easy/difficult was it for another person to understand the inputs, outputs, and process steps you identified?

- Did your partner's perspective help you clarify the SIPOC?

- How can the SIPOC help you establish a common understanding of scope with your project team and sponsor?

Facilitator Notes

Another version of this exercise will be used in the process documentation section of this book (Chapter 7).

SIPOC Worksheet

Process Name _____

List the inputs required to perform the process and the suppliers of those inputs. (Use another sheet of paper if more room is required.)

Supplier	*Input*

Process Start Event/Trigger _____

List the high-level activities required to perform the process (no more than 7).

_____

_____

_____

_____

_____

_____

_____

Process Stop Event/Trigger _____

List the outputs of the process and the customers for those outputs. (Use another sheet of paper if more room is required.)

Output (Product or Service)	Customer (User)

EXERCISE 3-4

World Hunger (Creating Scope Statements)

Description

Participants work in small groups to narrow an oversized problem statement.

Purpose

Teach participants to break down large, complex problems into manageable scope statements.

Time Required

20 minutes

Number of Participants

Groups of 3

Materials Required

None

Process

1. Arrange participants in groups of 3.

2. Tell the groups they are to solve the problem of world hunger. Their initial scope statement is the process of "feeding everyone in the world."

3. Tell them you recognize this scope statement is probably too big to address today and ask them to break this big scope statement down into 3 more granular scope statements. Allow 5 minutes for this task.

4. After 5 minutes, ask each group to select one of the smaller scope statements and break it down into 3 even more granular scope statements.

Discussion Questions

■ Was it hard to focus on the problem rather than the answers? How does that impact your ability to create workable scope statements?

■ Are the last scope statements developed the easiest way to address successfully? Why?

■ Is your team comfortable working with any of the scope statements? Why? If not, how much smaller would the scope statements need to be?

Facilitator Notes

■ Participants often move to answers and solutions instead of small subsets of the process or problem. Observe groups during the rounds and redirect them if they are on the wrong path.

■ Additional rounds may be added if participants are adept at creating more granular scope statements.

■ Typical scope statements from participants include production, distribution, geographic breakdowns, population control, etc.

■ This exercise can be repeated with any broadly defined problem and corresponding unmanageable scope statement.

Section 4
What Would Be Better?
Translating Customer Needs

EXERCISE 3-5
Dream Car (Finding CTQ Measures)

Description

A role-playing exercise that allows participants to practice translating high-level, expressed customer needs into measurable Critical to Quality (CTQ) product attributes.

Purpose

Provide participants with a learning environment to practice translating high-level expressions of need into measurable product attributes.

Time Required

30 minutes

Number of Participants

Groups of 3

Materials Required

None

Process

1. Arrange participants in groups of 3.

2. Tell participants they are automotive design engineers. They have been given instructions to design a car that is:

- Exciting

- Comfortable

- Prestigious

- Attractive

3. Ask them to develop measurable attributes of a new car that will fulfill these needs.

Discussion Questions

- Did your group find it difficult to agree on which attributes would fulfill a particular need?

- Do some attributes fulfill more than a single need?

- What needs not explicitly stated above are customers likely to have?

- Was it difficult to develop measurable attributes? Why?

- What techniques can you use to move from subjective to measurable descriptions?

Facilitator Notes

- Remind participants that measures may be either continuous (inches of room from floor to ceiling) or discrete (leather seating: yes/no).

- If participants struggle with the exercise offer the following examples:

  - Exciting attributes are often defined by acceleration (0 to 60 in x seconds), top speed, cornering ability, etc.

  - Comfort might be described by headroom, legroom, number of seats, lumbar support, and type of seats.

- Prestige can be defined by availability (restricted number of vehicles), exorbitant price, brand of manufacturer, etc.

- Attractiveness could be measured by customer survey results of various traits.

- Participants often define attributes that are not actually measurable. During the discussion, challenge them to define truly measurable attributes.

Chapter Four

How Is the Current Process Performing?
The Measure Phase

The opposite of "analysis paralysis" is "extinction by instinct." Six Sigma replaces intuitive decision making and performance analysis with disciplined gathering and the measuring of data.

Effective data collection is not indiscriminate but is instead carefully planned and organized around a set of questions to be answered or theories to be tested. Even with a well-focused data collection plan, time and resources will likely constrain the amount of data that can be assembled. Correct application of sampling procedures and statistical analysis can provide additional value against a limited data collection budget. Proper sampling techniques may also aid analysis and conclusions when collecting all the data is impractical or impossible.

Measurements, however, are only as good as the systems used to make them. In order to accurately measure process variation, measurement variation must be minimized. Effective use of data necessitates a validation of the measurement system. We need to be confident that the results of the measurement system are sufficiently precise, accurate, and stable.

Finally, after sufficient data is collected and confidence in the measurement system is established, an assessment of the current process performance may be generated. This first assessment serves as a starting point against which a modified process may be compared. The baseline assessment enables a measure of progress toward reducing defects and improving customer satisfaction.

This chapter includes games and exercises that demonstrate and teach the basic principles of data collection, sampling, measurement system validation, and performance baseline determination.

Section I
What Should We Measure?
Asking Questions and Testing Theories

EXERCISE 4-1

Unscrambling the Federal Reserve (Collecting and Organizing Data)

Description

Participants work together as a team to unscramble accounting issues at the Federal Reserve.

Purpose

- Improve participant ability to identify and utilize relevant data

- Teach participants to ask questions effectively

- Allow participants to test theories in a problem-solving context

Time Required

- Exercise: 30 minutes
- Debrief: 30 minutes

Number of Participants

Groups of 4 to 6

Materials Required

One instruction sheet and one set of 20 information cards for each team (see below).

Process

1. Divide participants into teams of 4 to 6.

2. Read the instruction sheet out loud to participants. Give each team an instruction sheet. Divide the 20 information cards evenly among the members of each team.

3. Explain that team members may not show each other their cards, but they may communicate freely otherwise.

4. Set a 30-minute time limit. Give time reminders at 10, 15, and 25 minutes.

5. Note starting time and ending time for each team. Score the results per the instruction sheet.

6. Post results for all teams to see.

Discussion Questions

Have teams debrief in their small groups.

- How did you organize the collection of data?

- Was there a process to get everyone's data into the discussion?

- How did you determine the relevance of data?

- How did time pressure affect the team?

- Once all the data was collected and organized, how difficult was finding the solution?

- What worked well?

- What didn't work well?

Facilitator Notes

- This is a fairly straightforward exercise to facilitate. Participants usually need very little assistance after the exercise has started. Almost all groups will find the correct answers.

- Successful teams typically use a matrix to organize data.

- In the discussion, focus on the type of data required, method of collection, and data storage/organization.

- If desired, ask each small group to share key learnings with the large group.

Unscrambling the Federal Reserve Instruction Sheet

The following 5 people are Federal Reserve Governors:

- Rob, Alan, Martin, Leslie, and Pat

The names of their regions, listed alphabetically, are as follows:

- Central, Eastern, Northern, Southern, and Western

The following reserve account numbers, listed in numerical order, have been issued to the governors:

- 551986, 4444582, 9866321, 87958997, and 23158884

The reserve accounts contain the following amounts (listed in descending order of size):

■ $800 million, $350 million, $200 million, $100 million, and $25 million

The regions are headquartered in the following cities (listed alphabetically):

■ Atlanta, Chicago, Detroit, New York, and San Francisco

Your task is to match the name of each person with the appropriate city, region, account number, and account balance.

If your team solves the problem correctly in every aspect, it will receive a score of 100. Each time a team turns in an answer that is not correct in every aspect, 10 points will be deducted from the team's score.

In addition, if your team turns in the correct answer before the 30-minute deadline, your team will receive 1 point for each minute you are early.

Unscrambling the Federal Reserve Information Card Data

Each of the following 20 pieces of data should be put on a card (1 piece of data per card).

■ Pat is not in the Southern Region.

■ The balance in account number 9866321 is $350 million.

■ Pat's headquarters are in Chicago.

■ Chicago is the headquarters for the Central Region.

■ Pat's account number and Alan's account number contain the same number of digits.

■ The balance in the Detroit reserve bank is less than $150 million.

■ The balance in Alan's reserve bank is $200 million.

- Alan is not in Detroit.

- New York's reserve account number is 23158884.

- Leslie is in San Francisco.

- There is a balance of $100 million in New York's reserve account.

- The reserve balance in the Eastern Region is $100 million.

- The Western Region account has 6 digits.

- Rob is not the reserve governor of the Southern Region.

- Rob's account number is 87958997.

- The balance in the Western Region reserve account is more than $100 million.

- Eastern Region believes the economy is slowing down.

- Western Region wants to raise its reserves to $1 billion.

- Pat drives a 1995 Explorer.

- Central Region headquarters are not in the downtown area.

Unscrambling the Federal Reserve Answer Sheet

Name	Region	Headquarters	Account Number	Amount
Rob	Northern	Detroit	87958997	$25 million
Alan	Southern	Atlanta	4444582	$200 million
Martin	Eastern	New York	23158884	$100 million
Leslie	Western	San Francisco	551986	$800 million
Pat	Central	Chicago	9866321	$350 million

EXERCISE 4-2

Who's Here? (Collecting and Displaying Data)

Description

Participants collect and display data to characterize a population and the smaller subgroups that view themselves alike.

Purpose

- Illustrate various types of data displays: histograms, dot plots, pie charts

- Demonstrate stratification of data

- Introduce concepts of central tendency, dispersion, and shape of data

Time Required

30–45 minutes

- Exercise: 20–30 minutes

- Debrief: 10–15 minutes

Number of Participants

Groups of 3 to 6; no less than 3 groups and no more than 6 groups

Materials Required

- Flip charts and marking pens (multiple colors)

- Who's Here instruction sheets (1 per team)

Process

1. Ask participants to divide up into groups of 3 to 6 with the people most like themselves with no more than 6 groups total. (Provide no additional information beyond "most like yourself.")

2. Provide each group with a flip chart and marking pens.

3. Ask each group to write a name for their team on the top flip chart.

4. Instruct the groups to record the team names of the other groups on their charts.

5. Distribute the Who's Here Instructions.

6. After all teams have written their question, instruct them to gather the data from all the other participants including their own team.

7. Make sure they record the individual responses and the team name of the respondent.

8. Instruct the teams to create a graphical presentation of their data and findings.

9. Ask each team to quickly (1 minute or less) present their findings.

10. Select a winning team (facilitator's discretion).

11. Debrief the exercise.

Discussion Questions

■ How did you decide on a question?

■ How would you characterize the data for all the participants? How would you describe the central tendency, dispersion, and shape of the data?

- What were the differences between the groups and how do they appear on the graphics? How did you highlight the data for individual teams?

- How useful are your graphics? How could they be improved?

Facilitator Notes

- The game is simple and straightforward, but some teams may need assistance in structuring a question that solicits data for a graphical presentation.

- This exercise is best run after a basic introduction to graphical presentations and formats.

Who's Here? Instructions

With discussion only within your group (no discussion with other groups), develop a single question that will be asked of each member of each team including your own. The question must solicit information that can be displayed graphically (histogram, dot plot, pie chart, etc.). The data will be used to characterize the entire room and also differentiate among the teams. Use only your visual observation, the team names, and your prior knowledge of the people in the room to develop the question.

You may not use the team names in your question and do not ask any question that is too personal to be discussed in public.

The winning team will have a graphical presentation which best characterizes how people decided to form groups "most like themselves."

Sample Questions

How tall are you in inches?

How many miles do you drive to work each day?

What department do you work for?

Which of the following best describes your personality?

- Sunshine

- Overcast

- Stormy

- Hurricane

- Blizzard

Section 2
Do We Need to Measure Everything?
Working with Samples

EXERCISE 4-3
Precision Delivery Inc. (Data Collection and Sampling)

Description

Project teams plan data collection and review sample results for Precision Delivery Inc. Exercise 4-3 may be used as a continuation of Precision Delivery Inc., Exercise 3-2.

Purpose

- Identify data collection requirements
- Identify potential sampling bias or measurement problems
- Apply the basic principles of sampling

Time Required

40–60 minutes

- Exercise: 30–40 minutes
- Debrief: 10–20 minutes

Number of Participants

Two or more groups of 4 to 6

Materials Required

- Precision Delivery Inc. Case Study (see Exercise 3-2)

- Project Proposal Description (use either a resulting Project Proposal from Exercise 3-2 or the PDI Project Proposal provided below)

- Data Collection Planning Sheet (below)

- PDI Sampling Data (below)

Process

1. Split into Project Teams of 4 to 6 people.

2. Instruct the teams to review the PDI Case and Project Proposal (or approved Proposal Worksheet from Exercise 3-2).

3. Give the teams 20 minutes to complete the Data Collection Planning Sheet for their project.

4. After 20 minutes provide the PDI Sampling Data to the teams.

5. Give the teams 10 minutes to review and discuss the provided sample data.

6. Debrief the exercise.

Discussion Questions

Have teams briefly describe their project, the type of data they plan to collect, and the questions they are trying to answer with the data.

- How will the sample data provided help your team?

- Describe any concerns your team has about the sample data. Is there any potential bias in the sample data? Is there a sufficient amount of data?

Facilitator Notes

- Remind the teams that they will need to measure variables related to process inputs, process activities, and output products or service.

- Remind the teams that their questions, when answered, should characterize the current performance of the process and potentially expose a root cause for their stated problem.

- Challenge the teams to establish a clear logical connection between the data they need and the question they want to answer. Ask how they would answer the question with a chart or graph of the data they collect.

PDI Project Proposal Worksheet

Team Name: Margin Makers

Project Title: Improve the PDI field operations process for package pickup and delivery.

Problem Statement: PDI gross margin is insufficient to sustain business operations and create growth. The current field operation process for package pickup and delivery results in sales rebates and idle time that degrade gross margin.

Goal Statement: Reduce sales rebates and idle time by 85%.

Business Case and Estimated Benefits: An 85% reduction in sales rebates and idle time will increase gross margin by roughly $11,000 per month and increase ROS to roughly 30%.

Benefit Calculations or Basis:

Prior month sales rebates = $9,400

Prior month idle time = $3,600

85% reduction = $11,050 per month

Executive Project Approval Board Use Only

Approval: Yes?   No?
Verified Benefits Amount: $11,050 per month in gross margin   ■   □

Data Collection Planning Sheet				
(1) Question to Be Answered	(2) Name of Data Required	(3) Operational Definition	(4) Related Measures (Stratification)	(5) Collection Plan
				Where: When: Who: How:
				Where: When: Who: How:
				Where: When: Who: How:
				Where: When: Who: How:

Directions

1. Write the question that needs to be answered by the data.

2. Write a name or brief description of the data.

3. Write a clear operational definition of the data to be collected.

4. Identify related measures or stratification factors.

5. Identify where, when, how, and by whom the data will be collected.

PDI Sampling Data

The following data is a systematic sampling of Field Operator trips for the past 2 weeks and represents roughly 5% of the total sales for that period.

Sample	Week	Day	Facility	Weight (lb.)	Miles (1 Way)	Time Slot	Vehicle	Minutes (1 Way)
1	1	Mon	S	3.5	13.8	AM	Bike	40.8
2	1	Mon	D	4.2	13.5	PM	Truck	54.1
3	1	Mon	D	4.6	13.4	AM	Truck	32.7
4	1	Mon	D	20.3	7.6	PM	Truck	28.6
5	1	Mon	S	21.6	11.2	AM	Bike	44.9
6	1	Tue	S	4.7	6.9	PM	Bike	21.3
7	1	Tue	S	19.2	6.0	PM	Bike	22.8
8	1	Tue	S	16.6	7.3	AM	Bike	24.6
9	1	Tue	S	9.1	14.7	PM	Truck	43.5
10	1	Tue	D	34.9	6.2	PM	Truck	25.1
11	1	Wed	S	42.6	0.4	AM	Bike	1.9
12	1	Wed	S	39.7	14.5	AM	Truck	28.5
13	1	Wed	D	48.8	0.2	AM	Bike	1.4
14	1	Wed	S	45.7	13.4	AM	Truck	26.2
15	1	Wed	S	19.1	14.4	PM	Bike	52.4
16	1	Thu	S	10.9	9.4	PM	Bike	31.5
17	1	Thu	S	20.2	3.8	PM	Truck	11.4
18	1	Thu	D	46.5	5.0	AM	Truck	11.9
19	1	Thu	D	28.0	7.9	AM	Truck	19.0
20	1	Thu	S	2.1	10.1	AM	Truck	20.4

Sample	Week	Day	Facility	Weight (lb.)	Miles (1 Way)	Time Slot	Vehicle	Minutes (1 Way)
21	1	Fri	S	40.4	5.5	PM	Bike	26.3
22	1	Fri	D	37.1	11.3	PM	Bike	52.7
23	1	Fri	D	37.3	3.1	PM	Truck	12.8
24	1	Fri	D	10.8	2.1	PM	Truck	8.4
25	1	Fri	S	26.4	2.1	AM	Bike	8.1
26	2	Mon	S	2.4	11.2	PM	Bike	34.8
27	2	Mon	D	47.1	12.7	AM	Bike	79.8
28	2	Mon	D	19.3	11.9	AM	Bike	45.1
29	2	Mon	S	8.0	9.1	AM	Bike	30.6
30	2	Mon	S	28.9	1.1	AM	Bike	4.4
31	2	Tue	S	14.9	4.4	AM	Truck	8.6
32	2	Tue	S	25.1	11.9	AM	Bike	46.4
33	2	Tue	D	5.6	11.6	AM	Truck	27.5
34	2	Tue	D	31.9	10.1	AM	Truck	25.6
35	2	Tue	D	20.9	3.3	AM	Truck	7.8
36	2	Wed	S	30.5	8.2	PM	Bike	34.9
37	2	Wed	S	1.1	9.1	AM	Truck	18.7
38	2	Wed	D	45.6	2.0	AM	Bike	9.3
39	2	Wed	D	28.6	2.4	AM	Bike	9.6
40	2	Wed	S	34.8	1.8	AM	Truck	3.6
41	2	Thu	S	30.9	13.9	AM	Bike	59.4
42	2	Thu	D	36.8	4.3	PM	Truck	15.8
43	2	Thu	S	37.7	0.5	PM	Bike	2.2
44	2	Thu	S	42.7	14.2	AM	Truck	28.6
45	2	Thu	D	17.5	10.2	AM	Bike	35.3
46	2	Fri	D	48.1	9.5	PM	Truck	39.8
47	2	Fri	D	11.3	14.8	PM	Truck	58.7
48	2	Fri	S	21.2	1.6	AM	Truck	3.3
49	2	Fri	S	10.9	6.0	PM	Truck	18.7
50	2	Fri	S	16.7	3.7	PM	Bike	14.0

Additional data for the past 2 weeks: 1,000 packages were picked up or delivered; 1 package was delivered to the wrong address, and no other formal customer complaints were received.

Section 3
Are We Speaking the Same Language?
Operational Definitions

EXERCISE 4-4
Super-Fine Peanuts (Applying Operational Definitions)

Description

Classification teams develop and apply operational definitions of premium peanuts for the Super-Fine Peanut Company (SFPC).

Purpose

■ Practice developing, documenting, and applying an operational definition for a classification measurement

■ Understand the impacts of operational definitions and measurement systems on project performance

Time Required

50–60 minutes

■ Exercise: Develop Operational Definitions   20 minutes

■ Inspect and Record Peanuts   20 minutes

■ Debrief: 10–20 minutes

Number of Participants

Two or more groups of 4 to 7

Materials Required

- Peanuts in the shell, 15 to 20 per group

- Empty egg cartons (1-dozen size), 1 per group

- SFPC Operational Definition Instructions, 1 per participant (see below)

- SFPC Inspection Instructions, 1 per participant (see below)

- SFPC Inspection Data Sheets, 1 per group (see below)

Process

1. Divide participants into groups of 4 to 7 members.

2. Provide the SFPC Operational Definition Instructions to each participant.

3. Provide 1 egg carton and 15 to 20 peanuts in the shell to each group.

4. Allow the teams 20 minutes to complete the SFPC Operational Definition Instructions.

5. Rotate the egg cartons and contents between teams (no team should have their own egg carton).

6. Assign 3 people from each group to be inspectors.

7. Send the inspectors out of the room.

8. Provide the SFPC Inspection Instructions and Data Sheet to each group.

9. Allow the teams 20 minutes to complete the SFPC Inspection Instructions.

10. Debrief the exercise when all teams have completed their inspections.

Discussion Questions

- What made the operational definitions easy or hard to write?

- What worked well or not so well in the operational definitions?

- How well did the inspection work?

- What kinds of problems did you observe?

- How could you use the Inspection Data Sheet information to improve the measurement system?

- How could the measurement system impact improvement projects?

Facilitator Notes

- Remind the teams to randomize the order of the inspections between the trials of each inspector.

- Remind the teams that inspectors should not perform their second set of classifications until the other inspectors have performed their first set. Don't have any inspector classify 2 sets continuously.

- Some teams may have problems keeping track of the peanuts by number or may experience data entry problems. Do not start over or attempt to help these teams. Record the data and report the problems in the discussion. Make the point that poor instructions or procedures are elements of the measurement system that must be addressed.

- With additional time, teams can use the data generated for Gage R&R analysis.

SFPC Operational Definition Instructions

1. Document an operational definition for a premium peanut using only the materials available in the room. Application

of the operational definition must preserve the peanut and the shell in original condition (i.e., no destructive testing, marking, opening, or tasting). A separate group of inspectors will use your operational definition to classify peanuts as either premium or subpremium.

2. Pick a group of 12 peanuts with at least 3 that would be classified as premium peanuts and at least 3 that would not be classified as premium peanuts (i.e., subpremium peanuts) using the documented operational definition.

3. Number the egg carton slots from 1 to 12 and place each of the 12 peanuts in a separate slot.

4. On a separate sheet of paper create a classification key that identifies each numbered slot as containing either a premium or subpremium peanut.

5. Write the name of your team on both the operational definition document and the classification key.

6. Place the documented operational definition and the classification key inside the egg carton with the peanuts and carefully close the carton.

SFPC Inspection Instructions

1. Bring an inspector into the room and provide the inspector with the SFPC Premium Peanut Operational Definition. (Do not provide the classification key.)

2. In random order, remove 1 peanut at a time from the egg carton for the inspector to classify as "premium" or "subpremium" and then return the peanut to its original egg carton slot after inspection.

3. Record the classification for each peanut in the SFPC Inspection Data Sheet.

4. Continue classifications until all 12 peanuts have been inspected.

5. Repeat the classification process (steps 1–4) with each inspector.

6. After all inspectors have classified the peanuts once, repeat the process to get a second set of classifications for each inspector.

7. After all inspectors have classified all 12 peanuts twice, transfer the classification key entries into the "Expert" column of the SFPC Inspection Data Sheet.

8. Bring back all the inspectors and review the results as a team.

SFPC Inspection Data Sheet

Peanut No.	Expert	A Trial 1	A Trial 2	B Trial 1	B Trial 2	C Trial 1	C Trial 2
1							
2							
3							
4							
5							
6							
7							
8							
9							
10							
11							
12							

Section 4
Are the Measurements Reliable?
Verifying Measurement Systems

EXERCISE 4-5
Object of the Game (Assessing the Measurement System)

Description

Participants take and record measurements for common desk objects in order to assess and improve a measurement system.

Purpose

- Introduce the concepts of accuracy, repeatability, reproducibility, stability, and resolution as applied to a measurement system

- Implement a simple measurement system and assess the types and sources of variation in the measurements

Time Required

20–30 minutes

- Exercise: 10–15 minutes

- Debrief: 10–15 minutes

Number of Participants

Groups of 5 to 7

Materials Required

- One irregularly shaped desk object per person in each group (e.g., coffee cup, door key, stapler, computer mouse, paper weight, beverage bottle, scissors, tape dispenser, telephone, etc.)

- One 12-inch ruler per person

- Paper and pen for each person

Process

1. Divide participants into groups of 5 to 7 members.

2. Provide each participant with a ruler, pen, paper, and 1 desk object.

3. Instruct participants to write down each of the objects in their group including their own.

4. Tell participants not to talk or communicate with other group members during the exercise.

5. Instruct participants to measure and record the length, width, and depth of their object without letting other group members see the recorded data.

6. Instruct participants to pass their object to another group member and again record the length, width, and depth without disclosure to other team members.

7. After all group members have recorded the length, width, and depth for all the objects in their group, instruct the participants to multiply the length, width, and depth of each object to arrive at a single value—the Desk Space Factor (DSF) for each object. Do not use calculators and remind the participants that no talking is permitted.

8. Instruct participants to turn over their paper and repeat the measurement process for all the objects without looking at their first set of measurements.

9. Debrief the exercise when all teams have completed their second set of measurements.

Discussion Questions

- How can we tell if our DSF measurement is capable of recording differences between objects?

- How consistent would the measurements be if we repeated this exercise tomorrow with the same groups and objects?

- What kind of differences do we see in the DSF metric for any given object? What do those differences tell us about the measurement system?

- How could we determine the "real" DSF for each object? What does the difference between the real and the measured DSF tell us about the measurement system?

- What are the possible sources of the measurement variation? How could the data help us improve the measurement system?

- When and why would improvement projects need to assess or validate a measurement system?

Facilitator Notes

- In order to obtain variation in the DSF metric keep the exercise moving briskly, limit communication during the exercise, and do not allow calculators.

- When participants request clarification on the measurements, replies should be vague or unresponsive. Likely question: "What do you mean by length, width, and depth?" Good responses: "If length is one direction and width is another, then depth is the third direction." "Length is how long, width is how wide, and depth is how deep."

■ The discussion questions should be used to introduce and illustrate the measurement system concepts of resolution, stability, repeatability, reproducibility, and accuracy.

■ With additional time the participants may define more clearly the measurements and procedures for the DSF. Participants would then repeat the exercise without the second set of measurements and check for improved accuracy and reproducibility within the group.

Section 5
How Good Is My Product?
Measuring Process Sigma

EXERCISE 4-6
Scrambled Letters (Measuring Process Sigma)

Description

Participants play a simple word game to generate data and develop a method for measuring process performance. This exercise may be used as a standalone exercise or a continuation of Scrambled Letters, Exercise 1-1.

Purpose

■ Demonstrate the concept of a defective product

■ Define an opportunity for defect

■ Define and calculate a simple measure of Process Sigma

Time Required

30–40 minutes

- Exercise: 15–20 minutes

- Debrief: 15–20 minutes

Number of Participants

Two or more groups with 2 to 5 members (equal group sizes are not required)

Materials Required

- Letter tiles (Scrabble tiles work well) or paper slips

- Bag or container for letters

- Flip chart or overhead display

- Watch or stopwatch (to time 20-second intervals)

- Paper and pencil

Process

1. Divide participants into groups of 2 to 5 members.

2. Provide paper and pencils to each group.

3. Read or display the "Rules for Scrambled Words" below.

4. Place all the letters in the bag or container.

5. Draw 9 letters randomly from the bag or container.

6. Write the letters on a flip chart or overhead display.

7. Start the timer and let the teams make words for 20 seconds.

8. Count down the last 5 seconds and announce "pencils down."

9. Ask each group to report aloud their words and number of unused letters.

10. Record the number of unused letters for each group on the flip chart or overhead display.

11. Replace the letters into the bag or container.

12. Repeat the random draw and word forming process 7 to 10 times.

13. Debrief the exercise.

Discussion Questions

- If the output product is a list of words and unused letters, how could we describe either a nondefective or defective product for this process?

- What is an individual defect?

- How many opportunities for defect do we have for each output?

- Calculate the yield and process sigma for each team.

- What other game goals could we create? How would we define a defect and calculate Process Sigma for these new output goals?

Facilitator Notes

- The time per round can be increased to more than 20 seconds, but keep the time short enough to maintain time pressure and produce variation in the results.

- Here is a suggested method of defining and calculating Process Sigma in this exercise:

  - A nondefective output has all acceptable words and no unused letters.

- A defective output has either unacceptable words or unused letters.

- An individual defect is any letter that is unused or used in an unacceptable word.

- There are 9 opportunities for defect for each output. (Each letter is an opportunity for defect.)

- Total Opportunities = Number of game runs times 9 opportunities per game run.

- Total Defects = Sum of all unused letters and letters used in unacceptable words.

- Yield = (Total Opportunities minus Total Defects) divided by Total Opportunities.

- Use the yield to find the Process Sigma in a Process Sigma table.

- With additional time, change the game goal and redefine defective, defect, and defect opportunity.

  - Add a goal for more than 1 word.

  - Change the goal to require exactly 3 words of any length and no unused letters.

  - Change the output goals to 1 word with 3 or more letters and the total unused Scrabble letter values more than 6 but less than 10.

Rules for Scrambled Words

1. Groups have 9 random letters.

2. Groups have 20 seconds to form words.

3. All words must be 3 or more letters.

4. Each of the 9 letters may only be used once.

5. Words may not be proper nouns or slang. (Decision of facilitator is final.)

6. Only a single list of words per team will be scored.

7. Game Goal: Fewest Unused Letters.

Example 1

Random Letters = P, B, F, S, R, E, S, A, M

Word List:

MESS

FAR

Result = 2 unused letters (P, B)

Example 2

Random Letters = D, G, O, P, R, E, T, A, T

Word List:

DOG

RAT

PET

Result = 0 unused letters

Chapter Five

What Are the "Deep Dive" Causes of a Problem?
The Analyze Phase

Now that we have defined the project and measured the baseline process performance, we're ready to hunt down and verify the root causes of the problem. We can map the process in detail, analyze the data, generate theories, design and run experiments, and finally, verify and quantify the candidate causes.

By mapping the process in detail we can discover bottlenecks, non-value-added activities, handoff problems, failure modes, and inconsistencies in performance. Analyzing data can reveal patterns and relationships for the process and product variables. Designing and running experiments allows us to take control of the process and produce data for selected process factors.

This chapter revisits 3 of the games or simulations introduced earlier to illustrate theory development, process analysis, data analysis, and design of experiment.

Section I
What Might Cause the Problem?
Developing Theories

EXERCISE 5-1
Scrambled Letters (Developing Theories)

Description

Participants play a simple word game to generate data and develop theories for process performance. This exercise is a continuation of Scrambled Letters Exercises 1-1 and 4-6.

Purpose

- Use basic data plots
- Identify theories for root causes

Time Required

45–60 minutes

- Identify Variables: 10–15 minutes
- Charting and Plotting: 25–30 minutes
- Discussion: 10–15 minutes

Number of Participants

Two or more groups with 2 to 5 members. (Equal group sizes are not required.)

Materials Required

- Recorded results from Exercise 1-1 or 4-6 (best if recorded in a spreadsheet, but a series of large visible flip charts is acceptable)

- Graph paper and pencil (spreadsheet or statistical software may be used if available)

Process

1. Divide participants into groups of 2 to 5 members (3 or more groups are preferable).

2. Provide paper and pencils (or computer software) to each group.

3. Ask the participants to call out the various types of available data from the Scrambled Letters game and record the list on a flip chart or overhead.

4. As a group, identify each data type as an input, process, or output variable, or as a stratification factor.

5. Assign each group one or more of the following analysis tools:

   - Time Plots (Run Charts)

   - Pareto Charts

   - Histograms (Frequency Plots or Dot Plots)

   - Scatter Diagrams

6. Ask each group to spend the next 30 minutes using the flip chart listing, data from the Scrambled Letters game runs, and their assigned analysis tools to develop theories on factors or variables that impact the process performance (number of defects).

7. Ask the groups to present their most promising theory for causes of defects. If a group has no promising theories ask them to present the causes they have ruled out and why.

Discussion Questions

- How did the plots or charts help your team explore the data and develop theories?

- How did stratification or classification of the data aid your analysis?

- What data did your team derive or calculate from the originally recorded raw data? How were derived or calculated data helpful?

- What additional statistical analysis would be useful?

Facilitator Notes

- At a minimum, record and have available the following data:

  - Game run order number (1, 2, 3...)

  - Input letters for each round

  - Unused letters by each group by round

- Ideas for additional data to collect:

  - Number of members in each group

  - Scrabble tile values of each letter

  - Number of words by group by round

  - Letters per word by group by round

  - Team demographic data (cumulative age, cumulative education, males and females)

- Most groups will develop multiple theories but the strongest evidence will support theories around the distribution of the input letters (number of consonants and vowels).

■ With additional time, statistical analyses (e.g., Hypothesis Testing, Regression) may be generated for various theories.

Section 2
How Does the Process Work?
Process Mapping

EXERCISE 5-2
Custom Landscapes at Affordable Prices (Process Analysis)

Description

Participants run a small business simulation producing customized works of art and then attempt to improve the process performance. This exercise is a continuation of Exercise 1-4.

Purpose

■ Introduce process mapping

■ Demonstrate value analysis

Time Required

60–80 minutes

■ Process Mapping: 20–25 minutes

■ Change Meeting: 15–20 minutes

■ Simulation Run: 15–20 minutes

■ Debrief: 10–15 minutes

Number of Participants

Groups of 8 to 10

Materials Required

- CLAAP Process Mapping Worksheets (see below)

- CLAAP Job and Customer Descriptions, 1 per person (from Exercise 1-4)

- Process Simulation Materials (per group)

  - Customer Order Forms (5) (from Exercise 1-4)

  - CLAAP Pricing Sheet (from Exercise 1-4)

  - Pens or pencils (4)

  - Box of crayons or colored felt pens

  - 12-inch ruler

  - Scissors (1 pair)

  - Construction paper, mixed colors (10 sheets)

  - Paper clips (3)

  - Glue stick or clear plastic tape

- Additional materials on hand for process change requests

  - Rulers

  - Scissors

  - Paper clips

  - Glue sticks or clear plastic tape

  - Blank name stickers or cardboard tents

Process

1. Review the CLAAP introduction (Exercise 1-4) with all the participants.

2. Divide participants into groups of 8 to 10 members (same groups as in Exercise 1-4).

3. Provide Job Descriptions, Customer Descriptions, and CLAAP Process Mapping Worksheets to each group. (Manager and Nurse are optional.)

4. Tell the groups they will have 20 to 25 minutes to prepare process maps and an additional 15 to 20 minutes to revise the process before they run the simulation again.

5. Instruct the groups to complete one CLAAP Process Mapping Worksheet for each of the following subprocesses:

   - Take Customer Order
   - Make Canvass
   - Apply Art
   - Frame Landscape
   - Calculate Price
   - Deliver Landscape

6. Remind participants to include all activities from the moment a customer approaches the CLAAP sales area to the time the customer departs with the landscape. Activities should also include handoffs between subprocesses and wait states.

7. Provide each group with the process simulation materials. (*Note:* A prestocked shoe box for each group is convenient and reduces preparation time.)

8. After all groups have completed their mapping and change meeting, start the simulation by asking the Bingo Parlor Manager to approach the Salesperson and submit an order.

9. Thirty seconds after the Bingo Parlor Manager approaches the Salesperson, ask the Art Dealer to get in line to place an order with the Salesperson. Thirty seconds later ask the Insurance Agent to get in line to place an order. Thirty seconds after that ask the Nurse (if available) to get in line to place an order.

10. Let the simulation run until all orders are filled and surveys completed.

11. Debrief the simulation.

Discussion Questions

■ Was the process mapping easy or difficult? Why?

■ How much of the process was identified as "no-value-added"?

■ Did any of the no-value-added activity remain in the process? Why?

■ How did the new process trial aid your attempt to verify theories?

■ How do the customers feel about the new process?

■ How would the changes impact the CLAAP business?

Facilitator Notes

■ Remind participants to map all the steps of the product moving through the process and not just the activities performed by each job description.

■ Most groups will find more than 50% of the activities are no-value-added, but for groups having difficulty, remind them to determine whether (1) the customers care about or are willing to pay for the activity, (2) the activity physically changes the product, and (3) the activity is the first try (not rework).

CLAAP Process Mapping Worksheet

Subprocess	Activity	Estimated Duration (Seconds)	Value-Added (VA) or No-Value-Added (NVA)

Section 3
How Do We Verify Causes?
Putting Data to Work

EXERCISE 5-3

Precision Delivery Inc. (Data Analysis)

Description

Project teams analyze data for Precision Delivery Inc., a pickup and delivery service, in order to find the root causes of poor operating margins. This exercise is a continuation of Precision Delivery Inc. Exercises 3-2 and 4-3.

Purpose

Use data analysis to identify, verify, and quantify root causes

Time Required

40–60 minutes

- Data Exercise: 10–15 minutes
- Data Debrief: 10–15 minutes
- Plots and Graphs: 10–15 minutes
- Plots and Graphs Debrief: 10–15 minutes

Number of Participants

Two or more groups of 4 to 6

Materials Required

- Precision Delivery Inc. Case Study (from Exercise 3-2)

- PDI Project Proposal (from Exercise 4-3)

- PDI Sampling Data (from Exercise 4-3; electronic format required if participants are to generate plots and graphs)

- PDI Calculated Data (see below)

- PDI basic plots and graphs (Figures 5.1–5.24 following)

- Spreadsheet or statistical analysis software (required only if participants are to generate plots and graphs)

Process

1. Split into Project Teams of 4 to 6 people.

2. Give each participant the PDI Case, PDI Project Proposal, and PDI Sampling Data (in electronic format if software tools are available).

3. Instruct the groups to review the data and identify additional useful data that can be calculated for each sample from the data provided (e.g., MPH, Revenue $, Rebate $, Margin $).

4. Debrief the data with the discussion below.

5. Distribute the PDI Calculated Data (in electronic format if software tools are available).

6. Distribute the PDI basic plots and graphs (Figures 5.1–5.24 following) to all the groups.

7. Instruct the groups to use the PDI basic plots and graphs to verify proposed root causes or develop new theories.

8. Debrief the PDI plots and graphs with the discussion below.

Discussion Questions

- Data debrief

- What additional calculated data would be useful? Why?

- What are your theories for the causes of low margins, price rebates, and/or idle time?

- How could we use the data to verify the root causes?

- Plots and graphs debrief

  - What are your conclusions about root causes?

  - Why are trucks better than bikes? Why are bikes better than trucks?

  - How does package weight impact PDI gross margins?

  - What factors would you use to predict the number of minutes required to travel to a customer for a pickup or delivery?

  - How could you use a prediction of trip minutes to improve gross margins?

Facilitator Notes

- The provided plots and graphs will not need to be distributed if spreadsheet or statistical analysis software is available, but additional time will be required for participants to generate their own plots and graphs.

- The underlying travel speed for this case is based on the following tables:

  - For a 25-pound package:

Suburbia	Truck	Bike
AM Slot	25 mph	15 mph
PM Slot	20 mph	15 mph

Downtown	Truck	Bike
AM Slot	25 mph	15 mph
PM Slot	15 mph	15 mph

- The bike gains 0.2 mph for each reduced pound and loses 0.2 mph for each added pound.

- The truck speed is unchanged by package weight.

- Random variation was applied to each individual run.

Precision Delivery Inc. Calculated Data

Sample	MPH	Fld Op($)	Idle Mins	Idle ($)	Revenue ($)	Rebate ($)	Margin ($)	USL	LSL	IN/OUT
1	20.3	10.20	0.0	0.00	8.55	0.00	-1.65	45	30	IN
2	15.0	27.05	0.0	0.00	9.23	9.23	-27.05	45	30	OUT
3	24.5	16.36	0.0	0.00	9.60	0.00	-6.76	45	30	IN
4	15.9	14.65	1.4	0.35	25.34	0.00	10.69	45	30	OUT
5	15.0	11.22	0.0	0.00	26.57	0.00	15.35	45	30	IN
6	19.4	6.41	8.7	1.09	9.74	0.00	3.33	45	30	OUT
7	15.8	6.60	7.2	0.90	24.18	0.00	17.57	45	30	OUT
8	17.9	6.83	5.4	0.67	21.61	0.00	14.78	45	30	OUT
9	20.3	21.73	0.0	0.00	14.15	0.00	-7.58	45	30	IN
10	14.7	13.78	4.9	1.22	39.91	0.00	26.13	45	30	OUT
11	12.0	3.99	28.1	3.51	47.58	0.00	43.59	45	30	OUT
12	30.6	14.61	1.5	0.39	44.70	0.00	30.09	45	30	OUT
13	10.4	3.93	28.6	3.57	53.83	0.00	49.90	45	30	OUT
14	30.8	14.04	3.8	0.96	50.70	0.00	36.66	45	30	OUT
15	16.5	13.10	0.0	0.00	24.09	24.09	-13.10	45	30	OUT
16	17.9	7.88	0.0	0.00	15.86	0.00	7.97	45	30	IN

17	20.1	10.36	18.6	4.64	25.22	0.00	14.86	45	30	OUT
18	25.5	10.47	18.1	4.53	51.54	0.00	41.07	45	30	OUT
19	25.1	12.24	11.0	2.76	33.01	0.00	20.77	45	30	OUT
20	29.8	12.61	9.6	2.39	7.15	0.00	-5.46	45	30	OUT
21	12.5	7.04	3.7	0.46	45.36	0.00	38.32	45	30	OUT
22	12.8	13.18	0.0	0.00	42.07	42.07	-13.18	45	30	OUT
23	14.7	10.71	17.2	4.29	42.30	0.00	31.60	45	30	OUT
24	14.7	9.61	21.6	5.39	15.78	0.00	6.17	45	30	OUT
25	15.6	4.76	21.9	2.74	31.40	0.00	26.63	45	30	OUT
26	19.2	8.70	0.0	0.00	7.44	0.00	-1.26	45	30	IN
27	9.5	19.94	0.0	0.00	52.05	52.05	-19.94	45	30	OUT
28	15.8	11.28	0.0	0.00	24.29	24.29	-11.28	45	30	OUT
29	17.8	7.64	0.0	0.00	13.03	0.00	5.39	45	30	IN
30	15.3	4.29	25.6	3.21	33.86	0.00	29.56	45	30	OUT
31	30.8	9.64	21.4	5.36	19.91	0.00	10.27	45	30	OUT
32	15.4	11.59	0.0	0.00	30.14	30.14	-11.59	45	30	OUT
33	25.3	14.37	2.5	0.63	10.62	0.00	-3.75	45	30	OUT
34	23.8	13.89	4.4	1.11	36.86	0.00	22.97	45	30	OUT
35	25.4	9.44	22.2	5.56	25.95	0.00	16.51	45	30	OUT

Precision Delivery Inc. Calculated Data (*Continued*)

Sample	MPH	Fld Op($)	Idle Mins	Idle ($)	Revenue ($)	Rebate ($)	Margin ($)	USL	LSL	IN/OUT
36	14.1	8.72	0.0	0.00	35.50	0.00	26.78	45	30	IN
37	29.2	12.18	11.3	2.82	6.13	0.00	−6.05	45	30	OUT
38	12.8	4.91	20.7	2.59	50.58	0.00	45.66	45	30	OUT
39	15.0	4.95	20.4	2.55	33.63	0.00	28.68	45	30	OUT
40	31.0	8.39	26.4	6.61	39.77	0.00	31.38	45	30	OUT
41	14.1	14.84	0.0	0.00	35.85	35.85	−14.84	45	30	OUT
42	16.1	11.46	14.2	3.54	41.82	0.00	30.36	45	30	OUT
43	12.6	4.03	27.8	3.47	42.74	0.00	38.71	45	30	OUT
44	29.8	14.64	1.4	0.36	47.75	0.00	33.11	45	30	OUT
45	17.4	8.83	0.0	0.00	22.53	0.00	13.70	45	30	IN
46	14.4	19.89	0.0	0.00	53.14	0.00	33.25	45	30	IN
47	15.1	29.35	0.0	0.00	16.34	16.34	−29.35	45	30	OUT
48	29.4	8.33	26.7	6.67	26.24	0.00	17.90	45	30	OUT
49	19.2	12.18	11.3	2.82	15.91	0.00	3.73	45	30	OUT
50	16.1	5.49	16.0	2.01	21.65	0.00	16.16	45	30	OUT

Precision Deliveries Inc. Basic Plots and Graphs

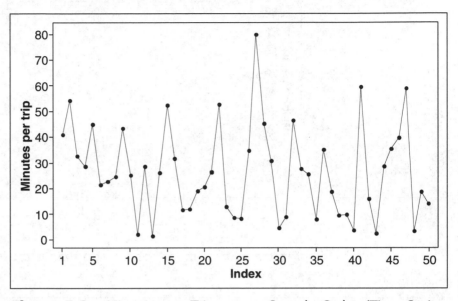

Figure 5.1   Minutes per Trip versus Sample Order (Time Series Chart)

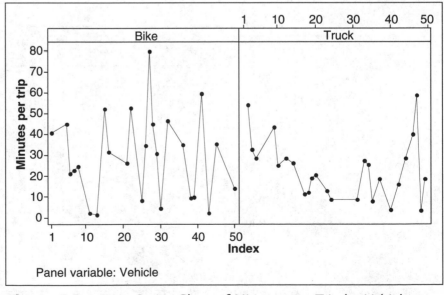

Panel variable: Vehicle

Figure 5.2   Time Series Chart of Minutes per Trip by Vehicle

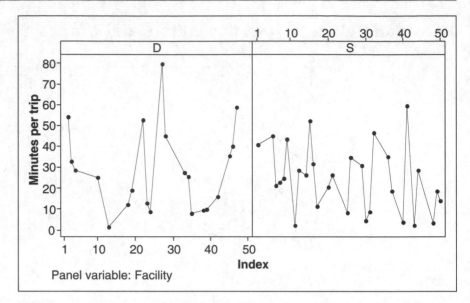

Figure 5.3   Time Series Chart of Minutes per Trip by Facility

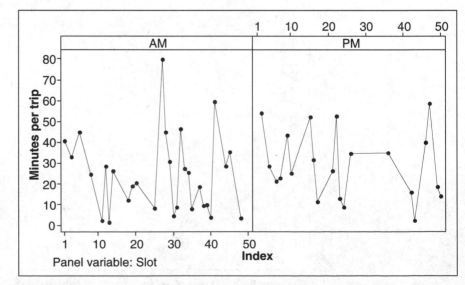

Figure 5.4   Time Series Chart of Minutes per Trip by Time Slot

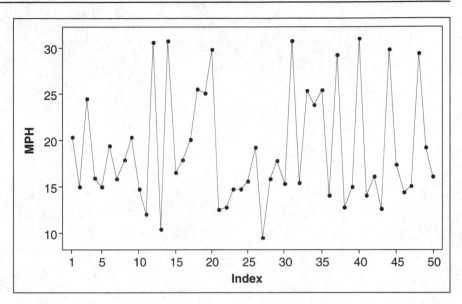

Figure 5.5 MPH per Trip versus Sample Order (Time Series Chart)

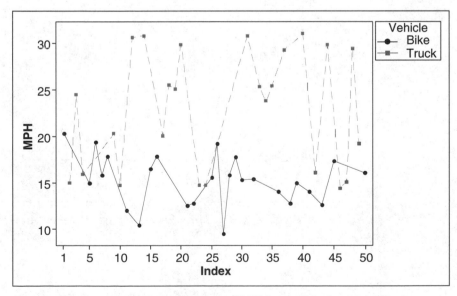

Figure 5.6 Time Series Chart of MPH per Trip by Vehicle

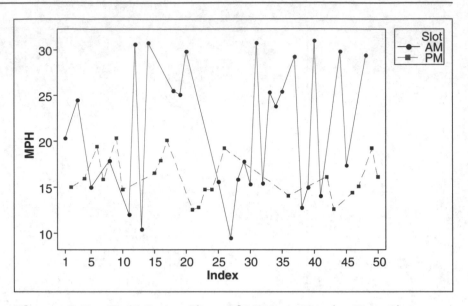

Figure 5.7   Time Series Chart of MPH per Trip by Time Slot

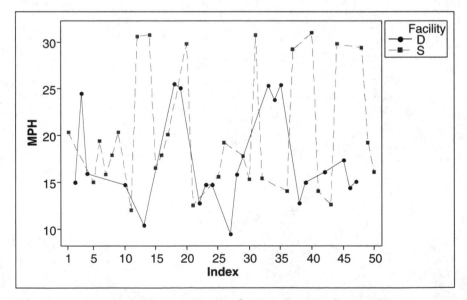

Figure 5.8   Time Series Chart of MPH per Trip by Facility

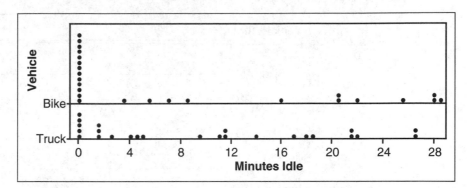

Figure 5.9 Distribution (Dot Plot) of Idle Minutes per Trip by Vehicle

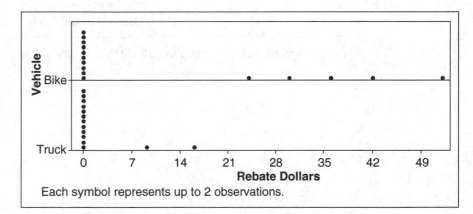

Each symbol represents up to 2 observations.

Figure 5.10 Dot Plot of Rebate Dollars per Trip by Vehicle

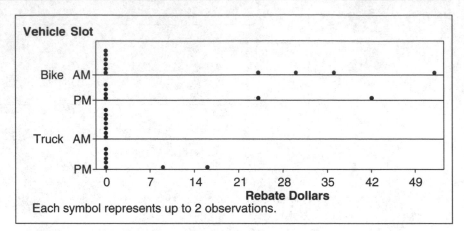

Each symbol represents up to 2 observations.

Figure 5.11 Dot Plot of Rebate Dollars per Trip by Vehicle and Time Slot

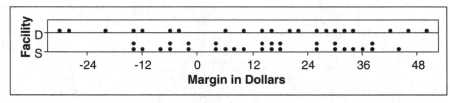

Figure 5.12 Dot Plot of Margin Dollars per Trip by Facility

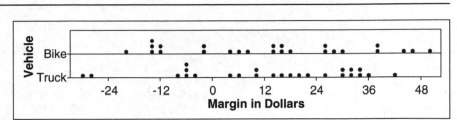

Figure 5.13   Dot Plot of Margin Dollars per Trip by Vehicle

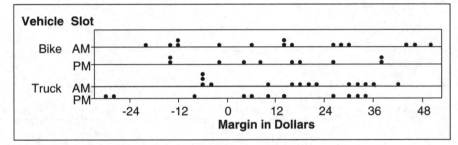

Figure 5.14   Dot Plot of Margin Dollars per Trip by Vehicle and Time Slot

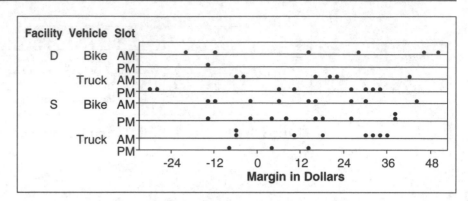

Figure 5.15 Dot Plot of Margin Dollars per Trip by Facility, Vehicle, and Time Slot

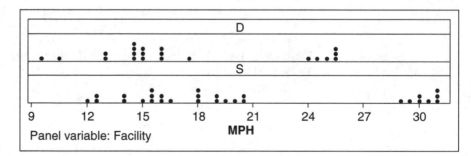

Figure 5.16 Dot Plot of MPH per Trip by Facility

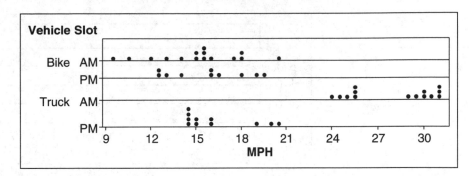

Figure 5.17   Dot Plot of MPH per Trip by Vehicle and Time Slot

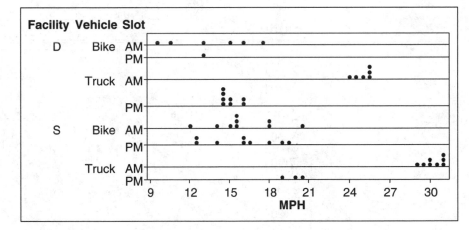

Figure 5.18   Dot Plot of MPH per Trip by Facility, Vehicle, and Time Slot

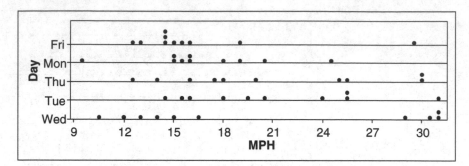

Figure 5.19   Dot Plot of MPH per Trip by Day of Week

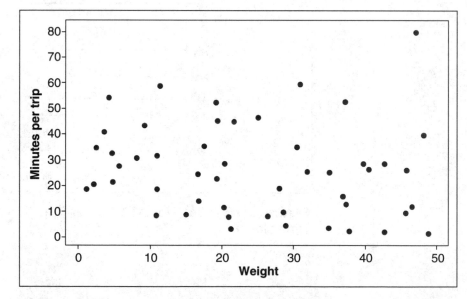

Figure 5.20   Scatter Plot of Minutes per Trip versus Package Weight

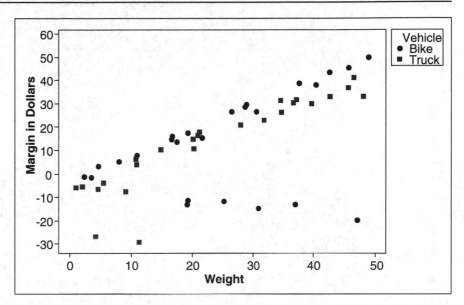

Figure 5.21   Scatter Plot of Margin Dollars versus Package Weight, Stratified by Vehicle

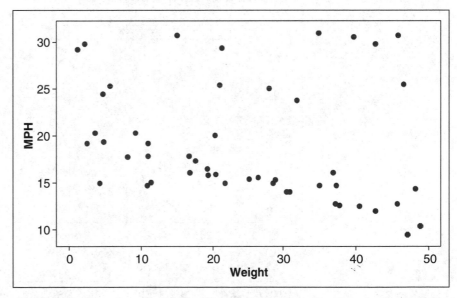

Figure 5.22   Scatter Plot of MPH per Trip versus Package Weight

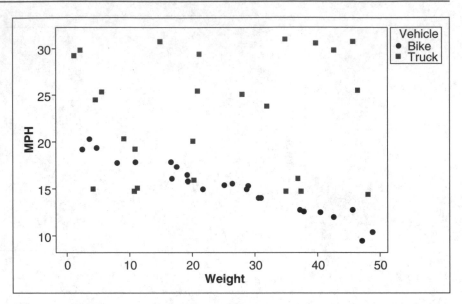

Figure 5.23 Scatter Plot of MPH per Trip versus Package Weight, Stratified by Vehicle

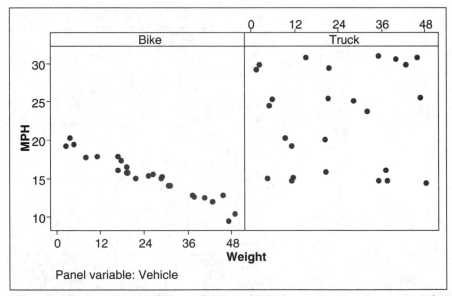

Figure 5.24 Scatter Plot of MPH per Trip versus Package Weight by Vehicle (Panels)

This concludes Exercise 5-3.

EXERCISE 5-4

Precision Delivery Inc. (Design of Experiment)

Description

Project teams plan and execute experimental runs for Precision Delivery Inc. to identify and quantify the impact of selected process variables. This exercise is a continuation of Precision Delivery Inc. Exercises 3-2, 4-3, and 5-3.

Purpose

- Prepare a Design of Experiment (DOE) plan

- Introduce the DOE concepts of factor and response variables, factorial design, run order, and randomization

- Illustrate the analysis concepts of main effects and interactions

Time Required

60–90 minutes

- Review case and project: 10–15 minutes

- Plan DOE: 20–30 minutes

- Debrief DOE plan: 10–15 minutes

- DOE simulation: 10–15 minutes

- Debrief DOE simulation: 10–15 minutes

Number of Participants

Two or more groups of 4 to 6

Materials Required

- Precision Delivery Inc. Case Study (from Exercise 3-2)

- PDI Project Proposal (from Exercise 4-3)

- PDI Sampling Data (from Exercise 4-3)

- PDI DOE Instructions below

- Margin Makers' DOE Plan and Results below

- Simulation model (see facilitator notes, required only if participants analyze their own DOE data)

- Spreadsheet or statistical analysis software (required only if participants analyze their own DOE data)

Process

1. Split into Project Teams of 4 to 6 people.

2. Give each participant the PDI Case, PDI Project Proposal, PDI Sampling Data, and PDI DOE Instructions.

3. Instruct the groups to prepare a DOE plan in accordance with the directions of Pat Hunter, CEO of Precision Delivery.

4. Debrief the DOE plan with the discussion below.

5. Distribute the Margin Makers' PDI DOE Plan and Results.

6. Instruct the teams to review the DOE results of the Margin Makers.

7. Debrief the Margin Makers results with the discussion below.

Discussion Questions

- DOE plan debrief

  - What questions are you trying to answer with your DOE?

  - What are the factors and response for your DOE?

- What settings will you test for each of the factors? Why?

- What order did you set for your test runs? Why?

- How will you use the results of your DOE to improve the PDI Field Operations process?

- Margin Makers' results debrief

  - Which factors impact miles per hour?

  - Are there any interactions between factors?

  - How could these results be used to improve the PDI Field Operations process?

Facilitator Notes

- A simulation model for producing results of experimental runs may be created in an Excel worksheet as described in these notes:

  - Enter the data in Figure 5.25 into columns A and B, rows 1–29. Leave column C blank.

  - Enter the data in Figure 5.26 into columns D, E, F, and G, rows 1–23.

  - Upon completion, format the column widths to make all entries and results visible.

  - If all data is entered correctly, a value of 19.999958 will result from the formula in cell G11.

  - The formula in cell G23 will display a value between 19 and 21, and will change each time the "F9" key is hit.

- The simulation model may be used to generate results for the DOE plan of each group and may then be used as the basis of the second debrief session.

	A	B
1	Input Variables	
2	Facility (D = Downtown, S = Suburbia)	D
3	Package Weight in Pounds (.1 to 50)	1
4	One Way Miles (Facility to Customer)	15
5	Time Slot (M = Morning, E = Evening)	M
6		
7	Process Variables	
8	Vehicle (B = Bike, T = Truck)	B
9	Dispatch Minutes Before Window Start	30
10	Window Minutes	15
11	Service Radius Miles	15
12	Field Ops Cost Per Hour - Bike	7.5
13	Field Ops Cost Per Hour - Truck	15
14	Price Per Pickup	5
15	Price Per Pound	1
16		
17	Output Variables	
18	Minutes To Customer (One Way)	=B4/B19*60
19	Average MPH (Road Time Only)	=G23
20	Trip Field Ops Cost (Round Trip With Idle Time)	=IF(B8="B",B12,B13)*(MAX(B18,B9)+B18)/60
21	Idle Time In Minutes	=MAX(B9-B18,0)
22	Trip Idle Time Cost	=IF(B8="B",B12,B13)*B21/60
23	Trip Revenue	=(B14+B15*B3)
24	Price Rebate	=IF(B18>(B9+B10),B23,0)
25	Gross Margin (Revenue - Rebate - Cost)	=B23-B24-B20
26		
27	Trip Time Upper Spec Limit	=B9+B10
28	Trip Time Lower Spec Limit	=B9
29	In or Out of Spec Limits	=IF(AND(B18>=B28,B18<=B27),"IN","OUT")
30		

Figure 5.25 Precision Delivery Inc. Spreadsheet (Columns A–B)

	D	E	F	G
1		Uncoded	Coefficient	Prediction
2		Value	Value	Value
3	Constant		21.352	=F3
4	Vehicle	=IF(OR(B8="B",B8="T"),IF(B8="B",-1,1),"ERROR")	1.14796	=E4*F4
5	Slot (S)	=IF(OR(B5="M",B5="E"),IF(B5="M",-1,1),"ERROR")	-2.5	=E5*F5
6	Weight (W)	=IF(AND(B3>=0.0001,B3<=50),B3,"ERROR")	-0.102041	=E6*F6
7	Facility (F)	=IF(OR(B2="D",B2="S"),IF(B2="D",-1,1),"ERROR")	1.25	=E7*F7
8	V*S	=E4*E5	-2.5	=E8*F8
9	V*W	=E4*E6	0.102041	=E9*F9
10	V*F	=E4*E7	1.25	=E10*F10
11	MPH			=SUM(G3:G10)
12				
13		Noise		Observation
14		0.2		Value
15	Constant			=F3
16	Vehicle	=1-E14+RAND()*E14*2		=E16*G4
17	Slot (S)	=1-E14+RAND()*E14*2		=E17*G5
18	Weight (W)	=1-E14+RAND()*E14*2		=E18*G6
19	Facility (F)	=1-E14+RAND()*E14*2		=E19*G7
20	V*S	=1-E14+RAND()*E14*2		=E20*G8
21	V*W	=1-E14+RAND()*E14*2		=E21*G9
22	V*F	=1-E14+RAND()*E14*2		=E22*G10
23	MPH			=SUM(G15:G22)
24				

Figure 5.26 Precision Delivery Inc. Spreadsheet (Columns D–G)

DI Design of Experiment Instructions

Pat Hunter has authorized no more than 32 trips of the Field Operators as test runs to aid your Six Sigma process improvement project.

You may control any or all of the following factors for each of the runs:

- Facility (downtown or suburbia)

- Package weight (lbs.)

- Distance to customer (0–15 miles, 1-way)

- Trip time slot (morning or afternoon)

- Vehicle (bike or truck)

- Dispatch time before window start (minutes; current default is 30)

In addition to the process factors, the Field Operator for each test run will record the following response data:

- Minutes to customer (1-way)

- Average miles per hour (road time only, does not include idle time)

Develop an experimental design and procedure for your process improvement project.

Margin Makers' PDI Design of Experiment Plan and Results

After mapping the PDI Field Operation process and reviewing the available data, the Margin Makers believe dispatch time is critical to minimizing both price rebates and idle time cost. To adjust the dispatch time, the team needs to have an accurate prediction of travel time to the customer location. They know travel time is a result of distance to the customer and speed (mph) of the Field Operator. They believe Field Operator speed may be determined by vehicle type, package weight, facility location, and time slot and have therefore designed their experimental runs to test these factors. If the team can successfully predict speed, they can choose the least expensive vehicle and adjust the dispatch time accordingly.

The team set up a full factorial experimental design with two replicates using Vehicle, Time Slot, Facility, and Weight as factors. They randomized the run order and recorded MPH as the response variable. Their results and analysis are shown in the following five tables:

1. Experimental Design and Results

Standard Order	Run Order	Vehicle	Time Slot	Facility	Weight	MPH
26	1	Truck	AM	Suburbia	50	30.2
30	2	Truck	AM	Downtown	50	24.2
21	3	Bike	AM	Downtown	0	19.8
32	4	Truck	PM	Downtown	50	14.3
14	5	Truck	AM	Downtown	50	25.4
3	6	Bike	PM	Suburbia	0	19.7
17	7	Bike	AM	Suburbia	0	20.1
9	8	Bike	AM	Suburbia	50	9.5
4	9	Truck	PM	Suburbia	0	19.8
8	10	Truck	PM	Downtown	0	14.2
10	11	Truck	AM	Suburbia	50	30.7
12	12	Truck	PM	Suburbia	50	19.2
15	13	Bike	PM	Downtown	50	10.0

1. Experimental Design and Results (*Continued*)

Standard Order	Run Order	Vehicle	Time Slot	Facility	Weight	MPH
16	14	Truck	PM	Downtown	50	14.7
18	15	Truck	AM	Suburbia	0	30.2
28	16	Truck	PM	Suburbia	50	20.3
19	17	Bike	PM	Suburbia	0	20.4
25	18	Bike	AM	Suburbia	50	8.7
2	19	Truck	AM	Suburbia	0	30.2
7	20	Bike	PM	Downtown	0	19.8
20	21	Truck	PM	Suburbia	0	19.9
13	22	Bike	AM	Downtown	50	12.5
23	23	Bike	PM	Downtown	0	19.7
24	24	Truck	PM	Downtown	0	14.7
22	25	Truck	AM	Downtown	0	25.4
11	26	Bike	PM	Suburbia	50	9.2
31	27	Bike	PM	Downtown	50	8.9
1	28	Bike	AM	Suburbia	0	20.2
5	29	Bike	AM	Downtown	0	20.1
6	30	Truck	AM	Downtown	0	23.8
27	31	Bike	PM	Suburbia	50	10.4
29	32	Bike	AM	Downtown	50	8.8

2. MPH versus Vehicle, Time Slot, Facility, Weight-Estimated Effects, and Coefficients for MPH (Coded Units)[1]

Term	Effect	Coef[2]	SE Coef[3]	T-Value	P-Value
Constant		18.594	0.1514	122.84	0.000
Vehicle	7.463	3.731	0.1514	24.65	0.000
Time Slot	−5.288	−2.644	0.1514	−17.47	0.000
Facility	−2.650	−1.325	0.1514	−8.75	0.000
Weight	−5.062	−2.531	0.1514	−16.72	0.000
Vehicle*Time Slot	−5.087	−2.544	0.1514	−16.81	0.000
Vehicle*Facility	−2.825	−1.413	0.1514	−9.33	0.000
Vehicle*Weight	5.163	2.581	0.1514	17.05	0.000
Time Slot*Facility	−0.175	−0.087	0.1514	−0.58	0.571
Time Slot*Weight	−0.087	−0.044	0.1514	−0.29	0.776
Facility*Weight	0.225	0.112	0.1514	0.74	0.468
Vehicle*TimeSlot*Facility	0.325	0.163	0.1514	1.07	0.299
Vehicle*Time Slot*Weight	−0.037	−0.019	0.1514	−0.12	0.903
Vehicle*Facility*Weight	−0.200	−0.100	0.1514	−0.66	0.518
Time Slot*Facility*Weight	−0.200	−0.100	0.1514	−0.66	0.518
Vehicle*Time Slot*Facility*Weight	0.250	0.125	0.1514	0.83	0.421

[1]Note: Standard deviation (S) = 0.856227; coefficient of determination (R-Sq, or R^2) = 99.18%; adjusted R-Sq value = 98.41%. [2]Coefficient. [3] Standard error of the coefficent.

3. Analysis of Variance for MPH (Coded Units)

Source	DF[1]	Seq SS[2]	Adj SS[3]	Adj MS[4]	F-Value	P-Value
Main Effects	4	930.38	930.384	232.596	317.27	0.000
2-Way Interactions	6	484.83	484.829	80.805	110.22	0.000
3-Way Interactions	4	1.50	1.496	0.374	0.51	0.729
4-Way Interactions	1	0.50	0.500	0.500	0.68	0.421
Residual Error	16	11.73	11.730	0.733		
Pure Error	16	11.73	11.730	0.733		
Total	31	1428.94				

[1]Degrees of freedom. [2]Sequential sums of squares. [3]Adjusted sums of squares. [4]Adjusted mean square.

4. Unusual Observations for MPH

Obs	Standard Order	MPH	Fit	SE Fit*	Residual	Standard Residual
22	13	12.5000	10.6500	0.6054	1.8500	3.06R†
32	29	8.8000	10.6500	0.6054	−1.8500	−3.06R†

*Standard Error of the Fit. †R denotes an observation with a large standardized residual.

5. Estimated Coefficients for MPH
(Using Data in Uncoded Units)

Term	Coefficient
Constant	21.1250
Vehicle	1.15000
Time Slot	−2.60000
Facility	−1.43750
Weight	−0.101250
Vehicle*Time Slot	−2.52500
Vehicle*Facility	−1.31250
Vehicle*Weight	0.103250
Time Slot*Facility	0.012500
Time Slot*Weight	−0.00175000
Facility*Weight	0.00450000
Vehicle*Time Slot*Facility	0.037500
Vehicle*Time Slot*Weight	−0.00075000
Vehicle*Facility*Weight	−0.00400000
Time Slot*Facility*Weight	-0.00400000
Vehicle*Time Slot*Facility*Weight	0.00500000

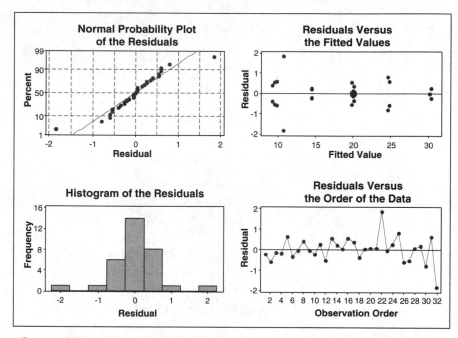

Figure 5.27 Residuals Plots for MPH Design of Experiment

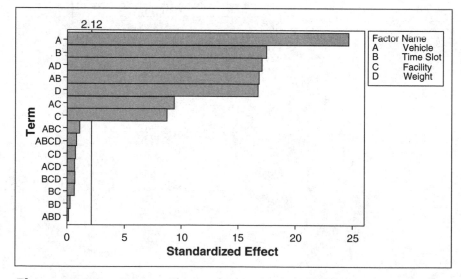

Figure 5.28 Pareto Chart of Standardized Effects for MPH Design of Experiment

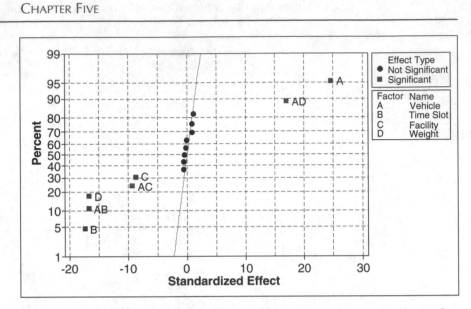

Figure 5.29   Normal Probability Plot of Standardized Effects for MPH Design of Experiment

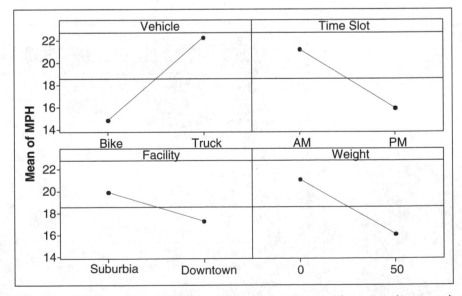

Figure 5.30   Main Effects of Vehicle, Time Slot, Facility, and Weight on Mean MPH

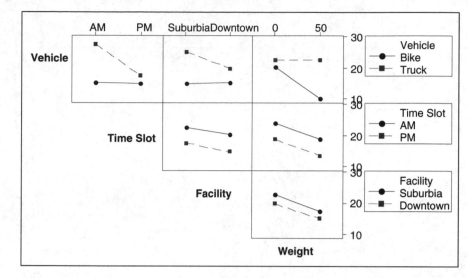
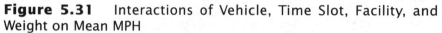

Figure 5.31 Interactions of Vehicle, Time Slot, Facility, and Weight on Mean MPH

Chapter Six

What Will We Change?
The Improve Phase

Proper application of Six Sigma demands new thinking. Start with the outrageous; find the kernel of truth in outrageous proposals and move to a wide range of practical, workable solutions. We can then use criteria and requirements to prioritize and select from the range of solutions. Pilot testing and risk assessment will shake out the problems before a full-scale deployment throughout the organization. Finally, we'll need to plan the implementation of the revised and tested process.

We don't want to be trite, but you do need to think "out of the box." This chapter includes exercises that will help participants identify novel ideas to address root causes, pilot test the solutions, assess risks, and plan the implementation.

Section I
How Do We Find Ideas?
Brainstorming

EXERCISE 6-1
Zoo Juggle (Brainstorming to Improve a Process)

Description

An easy-to-facilitate, mildly physical exercise where participants define a process by passing bean bag animals to each other in a particular order and then brainstorm and implement ideas to improve that process.

Purpose

- Encourage participants to think "outside the box" while brainstorming process improvement ideas

- Explore the dynamics of brainstorming and implementing ideas in a group setting

- Demonstrate how quality is defined by the client

Time Required

- 20 minutes for setup and exercise

- 20 minutes for debrief

Materials

- 3 bean bag animals

- Stopwatch

Number of Participants

10–25

Process

1. Ask participants to arrange themselves in a circle.

2. Throw 1 of the animals to a participant. Remember to which participant you threw the animal.

3. Ask the participant to throw the animal to another participant and to remember to whom they threw it.

4. Continue this until everyone has thrown and caught the animal once. Ask that no one touch the animal more than once.

5. When the last person has received the animal, have that person throw the animal back to the facilitator.

6. Tell participants that they have just defined a process. Ask them to repeat the process by throwing the animal from person to person in the same order.

7. Throw the animal back to the first person and have the group repeat the process.

8. Ask them to do it again and add a second animal to the process flow by throwing the second animal to the first person in the order immediately after that person has thrown the first animal on. Add the third animal before the first animal is returned to you.

9. Now that participants know that there are 3 animals, have them do it again. Start the process by throwing each animal to the first person as soon as that person has thrown the prior animal on. Challenge participants to complete the process as quickly as possible and time them with the stopwatch.

10. When all 3 animals have made their way back to you, explain that you are the client and their task is to pass all 3 animals in the same order to each person in the group. Tell participants that quality is defined by following the correct order, making sure there are no drops, and that they must complete the process as quickly as possible.

11. Tell them what their time was (to the tenth of a second) during their last process run.

12. Tell them you will time them for 3 more iterations and they must tell you when they want to be timed. (They may want to do "practice" runs.)

13. At each iteration, challenge participants to improve.

14. After they have been timed 3 times, congratulate them on their accomplishments and move on to the debrief.

Discussion Questions

- Were you satisfied with the results of your team?

- Do you believe your definition of "quality" met the quality standard set by the client?

- What "breakthrough" thoughts allowed your team to improve the most?

- What did your team do that encouraged new ideas?

- What did your team do that discouraged new ideas?

- Were all ideas considered or were any ideas ignored or passed over?

- How is the brainstorming environment in this exercise similar or different from the Six Sigma projects you are working on?

Facilitator Notes

■ For safety purposes, remind participants to make sure the person they are throwing the animal to has their attention before they throw it.

■ During brainstorming, some participants will be concerned with meeting quality standards and will ask for "rule" clarifications. If asked, just reiterate the instructions you have already given. This allows the group to experience the dynamics of one person viewing rules and definitions of quality differently than another.

■ In general, allow the group to determine if they have met the quality standards. The facilitator should only overrule the group for the most egregious violations.

■ Encourage participants to take time to plan if they do not do so.

■ Observe whether all ideas are considered or if some are ignored. Often, some quiet people have very good ideas, but are ignored because louder participants dominate the brainstorming sessions.

■ Almost all teams reduce errors and decrease their times at each iteration.

■ Some have been very creative and have completed the process in just a few seconds.

Section 2
How Do We Move from Impractical to Ingenious?
Generating Creative Solutions

EXERCISE 6-2
Creative Juicer (Generating Creative Solutions)

Description

In this exercise participants use a variety of creative thinking techniques (reverse thinking, random word association, and metaphors) in conjunction with supportive and critical thinking to generate ideas to solve a particular problem.

Purpose

- Teach participants to use creative thinking techniques through practice and experience

- Help participants understand the impact of supportive and critical thinking on idea generation

Time Required

- Exercise: 45 minutes

- Debrief: 30 minutes

Number of Participants

Groups of 3 to 7

Materials Required

- Cup

- Slips of paper with words on them

Process

1. Arrange participants in small groups of 3 to 7.

2. Ask each group to select a recorder.

3. Present the groups with a problem to solve. Some examples:

   - Freeway congestion

   - The rising cost of health care

   - Rainforest destruction

   The groups will do 3 idea generation sessions using 3 different creative thinking techniques and 3 different feedback processes. Allow 15 minutes for each session.

Session 1: Reverse Thinking and No Feedback

Ask participants to brainstorm and record creative solutions by using the "reverse thinking" technique. Explain that *reverse thinking* is using thoughts about how to make the problem worse in order to generate ideas about how to make it better. For instance, to solve freeway congestion, you would generate ideas on how to make freeway congestion worse. Then, you would see if those ideas inspire any creative ideas on how to make it better. Also, tell participants that they are not allowed to provide any feedback, positive or negative, on the ideas that are generated. Tell them they have 15 minutes to make a list of creative solutions using this technique.

At the end of the time allowed, ask participants to stop the discussions and put aside their list of solutions.

Session 2: Random Word Association and Critical Feedback

Ask participants to brainstorm and record creative solutions by using the "random word association" technique. Explain that *random word association* involves using a randomly selected word to generate creative solutions. Let's say you use the word *book*. You would then list all of the attributions or associations that the word *book* brings to mind. The next step is to see how each of the items on your list might apply to the problem. Also, tell participants that they are allowed to provide critical feedback (why the idea won't work) on ideas that are generated. Tell them they have 15 minutes to make a list of creative solutions using this technique.

Put slips of paper with a word on each in a cup and have each group pick a word. The words should be nouns. Here are some examples:

Egg	Cup
Book	Cardboard
Water	Wheel
Banana	Pebble
Picture	Building

At the end of the time allowed, ask participants to stop discussions and put aside their list of solutions.

Session 3: Using Metaphors and Supportive Feedback

Ask each group to brainstorm and record creative solutions by using the "metaphor" technique. Explain that the *metaphor* technique is thinking of metaphors (our problem is like...) for your problem in order to generate ideas about how to make it better. For instance, to solve freeway congestion, you might think "a freeway is like a river." Then you would think about how rivers flow and see if it inspires any ideas about improving freeway congestion. Also, tell participants that they are only allowed to provide supportive feedback (why the idea will work) on the ideas that are generated. Tell them they have 15 minutes to make a list of creative solutions using this technique.

At the end of the time allowed, ask participants to stop discussions and put aside their list of solutions.

Discussion Questions

Debrief in small groups:

- Which solution list is the most creative?

- Which solutions have the most potential to actually solve the problem?

- How effectively did each creative thinking technique produce solutions?

- How did the feedback rule in force during each session affect the results?

Facilitator Notes

- This exercise can be done using real problems the participants are currently facing. However, participants are typically more open to learning new ways of thinking (i.e., creatively) if they are discussing something that is more abstract rather than something for which they are personally accountable.

- As an alternative, you can assign different problems to different groups or different problems for each technique.

- During the idea generation sessions, observe the groups and enforce the feedback rule applicable to each session.

- As an alternative for the "random word association" session, you can ask the groups to look at a newspaper (if available) and use the first word (it should be a noun) they see. It is important that they use the first word so it is truly random.

■ Observe how quickly negative, critical thinking surfaces when groups discuss which solutions can actually solve the problem. Share your observations with the groups.

■ As an additional debrief, you can have each small group share their debrief answers with the large group. This is especially helpful if some of the small groups have difficulty generating ideas.

Section 3
How Do We Work Out the Kinks?
Piloting and Assessing Risk

EXERCISE 6–3
Well, Well, Well (Data Collection, Piloting, and Risk Assessment)

Description

Small teams compete to maximize the profits of Well, Well, Well (WWW), a well-drilling company, by collecting field data and piloting drilling instructions.

Purpose

■ Demonstrate the value of collecting data and piloting solutions before full-scale implementation

■ Recognize the relationship of data collection and pilot testing to the business case and risk assessment

Time Required

40–60 minutes

- Exercise: 30–40 minutes
- Debrief: 10–20 minutes

Number of Participants

Groups of 3 to 6

Materials Required

- Consultant Instructions below (1 per team member)
- Data Collection Sheets below (1 per team)
- Pilot Test Sheets below (1 per team)
- Sales Rollout Sheets below (1 per team)
- Results Sheet below (1 per team)
- Key Holder Instructions below (1 per Key Holder)
- Answer Key For Timbuktu Parcels below (1 per Key Holder)

Process

1. Split participants into groups of 3 to 6.

2. Remove 1 person from each team to serve as the Key Holder.

3. Distribute the Consultant Instructions to each team member.

4. Distribute a Data Collection Sheet, Pilot Test Sheet, and Sales Rollout Sheet to each team.

5. Distribute the Key Holder Instructions, Results Sheet, and Answer Key to each Key Holder.

6. Instruct the Key Holders to keep the Answer Key concealed.

7. Inform the teams that they have 30 minutes to follow their instructions and complete the exercise.

8. Debrief the exercise when all Key Holders have compiled results.

Discussion Questions

■ What strategy did your team use for data collection and pilot testing? Did it work?

■ How did the business case and risk assessment affect your data collection and pilot testing?

■ What would you do differently and why?

Facilitator Notes

■ Make sure all participants understand that each drilling results in either a $20,000 collection by WWW or a $15,000 payout by WWW. The $15,000 payout is not a partial payback of the $20,000 collection. Each parcel may have only 1 successful well. Any parcel with a failed drilling, a "dry hole," may be drilled again with either a Pilot Test or a Rollout drilling.

■ Walk around the room and ensure that Key Holders protect the data and understand the processes for providing data back to the consultant teams and calculating cost and revenue.

■ Have extra copies of Data Collections, Pilot Test, Sales Rollout, and Results sheets available.

■ Participants may be bothered by the elements of luck, but keep the discussion focused on tools, techniques, and trades used to understand and minimize the impact of known risk and chance.

Consultant Instructions

Rod Devine, owner of the Well, Well, Well (WWW) company, has hired your consulting team to maximize profits on a new sales opportunity in Timbuktu County. Timbuktu County has 16 parcels of land in need of well-drilling services. A well service contract generates $20,000 of revenue per parcel if the drilling successfully produces water. Each failed drilling attempt results in no collection of revenue and a contract penalty payment of $15,000 in damages to the parcel owner. A drilling will fail if the pump pressure is not correct or the drilling is not deep enough.

Your team is responsible for the Timbuktu County drilling operation and will submit Data Collection, Pilot Test, and Sales Rollout sheets to your local Key Holder. The Key Holder will return the sheets with data and cost results.

Prior rollouts in similar counties have produced average gross margins of $6,000 per parcel. Rod Devine has agreed to continue buying your consulting services only if the Timbuktu rollout produces an average gross margin greater than $6,000 per parcel.

Operating costs are as follows:

Soil Type Reading $1,000 per parcel

Devine Reading $2,000 per parcel

Sonogram Reading $1,000 per parcel

Pilot Test Drilling $100 per foot

Production Drilling $40 per foot

Soil type and Devine readings have been used together to determine the correct pump pressure and a minimum drill depth, but they must be calibrated to each new county. Historically, WWW has predicted pump pressure with great success, but poor predictions of drill depth have resulted in penalty payments or excessive operating costs. WWW has recently added sonogram readings to the available data collection. The sonograms are believed to provide an estimated water depth reading within 20% of the actual depth, but have not yet been proven in the field.

Your consulting team may make multiple data collection requests or run multiple pilot tests in any order and at any time prior to submission of the Sales Rollout Sheet. The Sales Rollout Sheet is submitted only once as the last action of your consulting team. The Sales Rollout Sheet must include drilling instructions for all parcels that do not have a successful well. Do not include parcels with successful pilot test wells on the Sales Rollout Sheet. Sales Rollout Sheets may not be modified after submission.

Key Holder Instructions

Observe the process and behavior of your assigned consulting team. Do not disclose any of the Answer Key information unless requested on the proper form.

Upon receipt of the Data Collection Sheet:

1. Look up requested data (checked boxes) in Answer Key.

2. Enter requested data into Data Collection Sheet.

3. Return the Data Collection Sheet to the consulting team.

4. Calculate and post the Data Cost after all data collection is complete (upon receipt of the Sales Rollout Sheet).

Upon receipt of the Pilot Test Sheet:

1. Check the Drill Depth and Pressure Setting columns against the Answer Key for the identified parcel.

2. If the Pressure Setting matches the Answer Key and the Drill Depth is equal to or greater than the Minimum Drill Depth, enter *Water* in the Result column.

3. If the Pressure Setting does not match the Answer Key or the Drill Depth is less than the Minimum Drill Depth on the Answer Key, enter *Dry Hole* in the Result column.

4. In the $ Revenue Column, enter $20,000 if the Result is Water.

5. In the $ Revenue Column, enter -$15,000 if the Result is Dry Hole.

6. Calculate the Drill Cost by multiplying the Drill Depth by $100/ft and enter the Drill Cost for the parcel.

7. Return the Sheet to the consulting team.

Upon receipt of the Sales Rollout Sheet:

1. On the Sales Rollout sheet, eliminate parcels that had successful wells (Result = Water) in Pilot Testing.

2. Request any missing Drill Depth and Pressure Setting data for parcels without a successful well (Result = *Darthole*) in Pilot Testing.

3. Check the Drill Depth and Pressure Setting columns against the Answer Key for the identified parcel.

4. If the Pressure Setting matches the Answer Key and the Drill Depth is equal to or greater than the Minimum Drill Depth, enter *Water* in the Result column.

5. If the Pressure Setting does not match the Answer Key or the Drill Depth is less than the Minimum Drill Depth on the Answer Key, enter *Dry Hole* in the Result column.

6. In the $ Revenue column, enter $20,000 if the Result is Water.

7. In the $ Revenue column, enter -$15,000 if the Result is Dry Hole.

8. Calculate the Drill Cost by multiplying the Drill Depth by $40/ft and enter the Drill Cost for the parcel.

9. Complete the Results Sheet by entering the totals from the Data Collection, Pilot Testing, and Rollout Sheets.

Data Collection Sheet

Directions: Use the check boxes to request data by parcel.
Calculate the Data Cost for each parcel by adding $1,000
per parcel for Soil Type readings, $2,000 per parcel for
Devine readings, and $1,000 per parcel for Sonogram
readings.

Parcel Address	Soil Type (R=Rock, S=Sand)	Devine Reading (W = Weak, S = Strong)	Sonogram Reading (Water Depth)	Data Cost ($)
A1	❏	❏	❏	
A2	❏	❏	❏	
A3	❏	❏	❏	
A4	❏	❏	❏	
B1	❏	❏	❏	
B2	❏	❏	❏	
B3	❏	❏	❏	
B4	❏	❏	❏	
C1	❏	❏	❏	
C2	❏	❏	❏	
C3	❏	❏	❏	
C4	❏	❏	❏	
D1	❏	❏	❏	
D2	❏	❏	❏	
D3	❏	❏	❏	
D4	❏	❏	❏	
			Total	

Pilot Test Sheet

Directions: Use the check boxes to request a pilot test by parcel. Calculate the Drill Cost for each parcel pilot by multiplying the drill depth in feet by $100/ft. After the test results are determined enter $20,000 in the Revenue column for a successful test (water) or –$15,000 for an unsuccessful test (dry hole).

Parcel Address	Drill Depth (50–150 ft)	Pressure Setting (Low, High)	Test Result (Dry Hole, Water)	Drill Cost ($100/ft)	$ Revenue (Penalty)
❑ A1					
❑ A2					
❑ A3					
❑ A4					
❑ B1					
❑ B2					
❑ B3					
❑ B4					
❑ C1					
❑ C2					
❑ C3					
❑ C4					
❑ D1					
❑ D2					
❑ D3					
❑ D4					
			Total		

Sales Rollout Sheet

Directions: Enter a drill depth and pressure setting for all parcels that do not have a successful pilot test well. Calculate the Drill Cost for each parcel by multiplying the drill depth in feet by $40/ft. After the results are determined, enter $20,000 in the Revenue column for a successful drilling (water) or –$15,000 for an unsuccessful drilling (dry hole).

Parcel Address	Drill Depth (50–150 ft)	Pressure Setting (Low, High)	Result (Dry Hole, Water)	Drill Cost ($40/ft)	$ Revenue (Penalty)
A1					
A2					
A3					
A4					
B1					
B2					
B3					
B4					
C1					
C2					
C3					
C4					
D1					
D2					
D3					
D4					
			Total		

Results Sheet

Directions: Enter results from the Data Collection, Pilot Test, and Sales Rollout sheets.

Revenue (Net Penalties) from Pilot Tests	
Revenue (Net Penalties) from Sales Rollouts	
Total Revenue (Net Penalties)	
Data Collection Cost	
Pilot Drilling Cost	
Rollout Drilling Cost	
Total Cost	
Gross Margin (Total Revenue Less Total Cost)	
Avg. Margin Per Parcel (Gross Margin/16 Parcels)	

Answer Key for Timbuktu County

Parcel Address	Soil Type	Devine Reading	Sonogram Reading	Pressure Setting	Minimum Drill Depth (ft)
A1	Sand	Strong	45	High	60
A2	Sand	Strong	55	High	65
A3	Sand	Strong	65	High	65
A4	Sand	Strong	75	High	60
B1	Sand	Weak	120	Low	100
B2	Sand	Weak	110	Low	105
B3	Sand	Weak	90	Low	100
B4	Sand	Weak	80	Low	105
C1	Rock	Strong	70	Low	85
C2	Rock	Strong	75	Low	80
C3	Rock	Strong	80	Low	85
C4	Rock	Strong	85	Low	80
D1	Rock	Weak	90	High	120
D2	Rock	Weak	110	High	120
D3	Rock	Weak	130	High	125
D4	Rock	Weak	150	High	125

Section 4
How Do We Put Solutions in place?
Implementation Planning

EXERCISE 6-4

Cube Puzzle (Implementation Planning)

Description

Participants work to solve a 3-dimensional puzzle by taking turns handling the problem.

Purpose

- Explore the dynamics of effective team problem solving

- Explore implementation issues such as planning, openness to new ideas and breaking with existing processes, role clarity, shared ownership of problems, effective use of resources, and communication

Time Required

30–60 minutes, depending on the number of participants

Number of Participants

Groups of 3 to 10

Materials Required

Cube puzzle—a popular puzzle that consists of 27 small cubes that are joined together and that must be manipulated into a larger cube that is a 3 by 3 construction of the smaller cubes (or any other single-piece, hands-on, 3-dimensional puzzle)

Process

1. Show cube and define goal (goal is to put cube back into form).

2. Undo cube and jumble it. Place on table in front of group.

3. Rules:

   ■ Each person may only handle the cube during his or her turn.

   ■ Each person must take a turn in an order determined by the group. That order may not change once it is set.

   ■ Each turn may last no longer than one minute.

4. Allow 5 minutes for planning time. The group may not touch the puzzle during this time.

5. Keep rotating until the puzzle is complete or time is over.

Discussion Questions

■ Did the group come to clear agreement on an implementation plan?

■ Did they stick to the plan?

■ Did the group assign roles? Were they effective?

■ How did the group make decisions?

■ Were all suggestions considered?

■ Did the group share learning by each member?

■ Did the group share ownership of the problem or did ownership rotate with the puzzle?

■ How willing were people to undo someone else's work?

- How was the problem-solving process the group displayed similar or dissimilar to problem solving on Six Sigma projects?

Facilitator Notes

- This game can be done with a variety of 3-dimensional puzzles. The puzzles should be difficult, but solvable by most people within a limited timeframe. A Rubik's Cube is far too difficult for this exercise.

- It may be helpful to act as an observer or to assign observers to each team if you have multiple groups. Use the discussion questions as guidelines for observers.

- In general, you should allow enough time for each person on the team to handle the puzzle several times.

- Most teams do not complete the puzzle. One way teams have completed the puzzle is to have only a single team member work on it. Each time that person's minute is up, all of the other team members quickly touch the puzzle and return it to their puzzle solver.

- We have also observed that some team members become disengaged during the time they are not handling the puzzle.

- This is a rich exercise and almost all observed behaviors easily tie directly back to Six Sigma implementations.

Chapter Seven

Are We There Yet?
The Control Phase

A key discipline of Six Sigma is capturing and maintaining gains. This entails making improvements permanent and continually measuring the results to determine if real improvement has been achieved. Organizational memory of improvement is short and expedient if not documented and standardized. The control plan must institutionalize change by documenting the revised process, monitoring the adoption, reviewing the results, and responding to new issues or problems.

This chapter includes exercises that demonstrate the documenting and standardizing of a process and the monitoring of process metrics and control charts.

Section I
How Do We Maintain the Benefits of Change?
Documenting and Standardizing

EXERCISE 7-1
Break It Down (Individual Process Documentation)

Description

In this process documentation exercise, individuals document a process and then receive feedback from another person on the clarity of their documentation.

Purpose

- Teach participants to define and articulate discrete steps in a process

- Demonstrate the dynamics of communicating a process to another person

- Demonstrate how processes can be more complicated than commonly perceived

Time Required

45 minutes

- 10 minutes for setup and completing worksheet

- 20 minutes for clarification coaching session

- 15 minutes for debrief

Number of Participants

Participants work in pairs.

Materials Required

Process Steps Worksheet (see below)

Process

1. Ask participants to think of a task or process with which they are familiar and proficient.

2. Introduce the Process Steps Worksheet. Explain that the participants are to list the inputs and outputs to the task/process and the steps required to complete the task/process.

3. Allow 5 minutes for participants to complete the worksheet. Provide a time update when 1 minute is remaining.

4. Have each participant select a partner to work with. Instruct each pair to take turns reviewing each other's Process Steps Worksheet and explore the following issues:

    ■ Did the worksheet clearly define start and end events?

    ■ Is the worksheet clear enough to allow someone unfamiliar with the task/process to complete the task/process?

    ■ How could the worksheet be more readily understandable, useful, and complete to someone unfamiliar with the task/process?

5. Allow 20 minutes for the discussion.

6. Halfway into the time allotted, remind participants to be good time managers and allow each person the opportunity for feedback.

Discussion Questions

Debrief as a group using the questions below (approximately 15 minutes):

- Was it easy or difficult to identify the inputs, outputs, and process steps of a task/process you are familiar with?

- How easy/difficult was it for another person to understand the inputs, outputs, and process steps you identified?

- Did your partner's perspective on your list of steps differ from yours or help you clarify the steps you take?

- How would you make the documentation more understandable and useful?

Facilitator Notes

- If participants are short on ideas, suggest tying a shoe or making a paper airplane.

- Participants often experience difficulty in explaining even simple tasks.

- Ideas that can improve documentation include graphics and pictures, flow charts, context, what to do in case of errors, and a clear description of the end state.

Process Steps Worksheet

List the inputs required to complete the task/process. (Use another sheet of paper if more room is required.)

_____

_____

_____

_____

_____

List the outputs of the completed task/process. (Use another sheet of paper if more room is required.)

_____

_____

_____

_____

_____

List the process steps required to complete the task/process. (Use another sheet of paper if more room is required.)

_____

_____

_____

_____

_____

_____

_____

_____

_____

EXERCISE 7-2
Snowflake (Group Process Documentation)

Description

In this process documentation exercise a group of people try to document a process well enough that another person can replicate the process.

Purpose

- Teach participants the importance of process documentation

- Teach participants to transfer process knowledge effectively

- Explore the strengths and weaknesses of written instructions

- Teach participants to create effective, detailed process documentation

Time Required

60 minutes

- 5 minutes for setup

- 15 minutes to design a snowflake and write instructions for replicating it

- 10 minutes for volunteer to re-create snowflake

- 5 minutes for solution of winning snowflake and awarding prizes.

- 25 minutes for debrief

Number of Participants

10 to 50 or more

Materials Required

- Paper

- Scissors

- Pens/pencils

- Prizes

Process

1. Organize participants into groups of 5 to 8 people. Ask for a volunteer from each group. This volunteer will be the observer for the group.

2. Ask for a second volunteer. This volunteer (snowflake manufacturer) will try to re-create the snowflake design.

3. Read these instructions to the participants.

   "The first step of this exercise is for each group of snowflake designers to design a paper snowflake by making cuts in a folded piece of paper. Snowflake designs will be judged by the criteria of complexity and aesthetic appeal. After the groups have designed their snowflake and created a prototype, they will develop a set of written instructions for their snowflake manufacturer. The snowflake manufacturer will be outside of the room during the design phase. The manufacturer will attempt to re-create the original snowflake design using only the written instructions. No talking is allowed during the manufacturing phase. The winning team will be selected based on the similarity of the manufactured snowflake to the prototype and the aesthetic appeal and complexity of their snowflake design."

4. Ask the snowflake manufacturers to leave the room. Have them convene in another room and spend the design time discussing a relevant question such as, "Who was the most effective teacher you ever had? Why?"

5. Provide paper and scissors to design teams. Tell them they have 15 minutes to design their snowflake and write their instructions. Remind them their designs will be judged for aesthetic appeal and complexity.

6. Ask observers to be completely silent during the design and manufacturing phases. They should take notes on how effective/ineffective the instructions were and how they could have been more effective.

7. After the design phase time limit is reached, invite the manufacturers to join their respective team of designers and use their team's instructions to create their snowflake.

8. Manufacturers are only allowed to use the written instructions to create their snowflakes. No talking or other assistance is allowed.

9. At the end of the manufacturing time or when all snowflakes have been manufactured, have the teams display their prototype snowflake alongside the manufactured snowflake.

10. Have all participants browse the snowflake displays and then have the participants vote for the snowflake team that has the best design and replication.

11. Award prizes to the winning team.

Discussion Questions

Begin debriefing in teams (20 minutes). Ask each team to identify 3 lessons learned from the exercise. Start the team debriefs by having the observers share their comments with the team they were observing. Then have the manufacturer comment on the process. Encourage teams to react to the observations by probing the observer and manufacturer for more information.

- How does complexity of a task affect the effectiveness of written instructions/documentation?

- Did the design team underestimate the difficulty of the task and writing the instructions?

- Did the design team and manufacturer have different perspectives on the effectiveness of the instructions?

- Did the design team provide the manufacturer with a mental or physical picture of the finished product or just give step-by-step instructions?

- What could the design team have done to make the documentation more effective for the manufacturer?

Close the exercise by having each team share their 3 lessons learned with the entire group (5 minutes).

Facilitator Notes

If applicable, you can note that process documentation provides the basis for process measurement.

Section 2
How Do We Measure Progress?
Keeping Score with Process Metrics

EXERCISE 7-3

Scrambled Letters (Tracking Performance)

Description

Participants play a simple word game to generate data and measure changes in performance. This exercise is a continuation of Scrambled Letters Exercises 1-1, 4-6, and 5-1.

Purpose

■ Illustrate a change in process performance

■ Introduce control charts

Time Required

30–45 minutes

■ Exercise: 10–15 minutes

■ Charting: 10–15 minutes

■ Debrief: 10–15 minutes

Number of Participants

Two or more groups with 2 to 5 members (equal group sizes are not required)

Materials Required

■ Recorded results from Exercise 1-1, 4-6, or 5-1 (best if recorded in a spreadsheet, but a series of large visible flip charts is acceptable)

■ Graph paper and pencil (spreadsheet or statistical software may be used if available)

■ Letter tiles (Scrabble tiles work well) or paper slips

■ Containers for letters (shoebox and two plastic bowls work well)

■ Flip chart or overhead display

■ Watch, stopwatch, or timer (to time 20-second intervals)

■ Sample Control Charts for Scrambled Letters (Figures 7.1, 7.2., and 7.3)

Process

1. Divide participants into the same groups of 2 to 5 members as in the original exercise.

2. Provide paper and pencils (or software) to each group.

3. Tell the groups they will be recording additional data for the Scrambled Letters game.

4. Run the Scrambled Letters game (Exercise 1-1) with the following changes:

   - In advance of the exercise, place the vowels and consonants in separate containers and don't let the participants see the separated containers. (A shoebox with 2 plastic bowls inside works well.)

   - Draw 4 vowels and 5 consonants randomly from the respective containers.

   - Return the vowels and consonants to their respective containers.

5. Instruct each group to create a time series chart for defects per run with both their original runs and the new runs. (Create a control chart if software is available.) Define a *defect* as any number that is unused or used in an unacceptable word. Start the debrief.

6. Hand out the Sample Control Charts for Scrambled Letters after asking the first 2 discussion questions below.

Discussion Questions

- How is your process performing?

- Is the process performance changing? Why?

- What are the Control Charts telling us about the process before and after the new runs?

Facilitator Notes

- The exercise works best with a minimum of 20 game runs for all the letters in a single container and a minimum of 12 game runs for the consonants and vowels separated.

- If software is available, allow additional time for the participants to create control charts using their own old and new game run data.

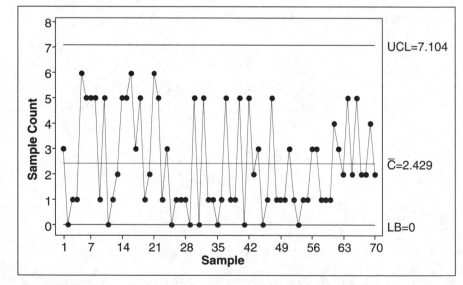

Figure 7.1   Control Chart for Unused Letters before New Runs

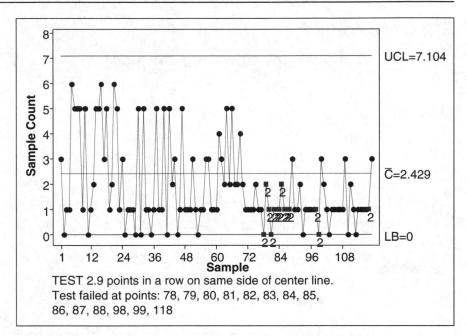

TEST 2. 9 points in a row on same side of center line.
Test failed at points: 78, 79, 80, 81, 82, 83, 84, 85, 86, 87, 88, 98, 99, 118

Figure 7.2   Control Chart for Unused Letters Including New Runs

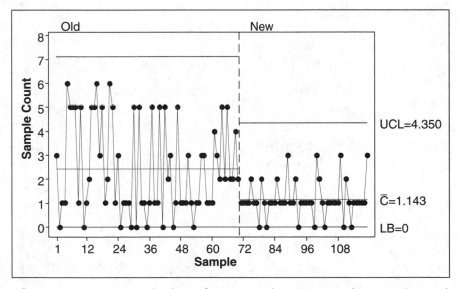

Figure 7.3   Control Chart for Unused Letters with New Control Limits

195

EXERCISE 7-4

Precision Delivery Inc. (Scoring the Goal)

Description

Project teams analyze data for Precision Delivery Inc., a pickup and delivery service, in order to assess a process change impact on the business.

This exercise is a continuation of Precision Delivery Inc. Exercises 3-2, 4-3, 5-3, and 5-4.

Purpose

- Use data to assess changes in process performance
- Use data to assess the status of the project business case

Time Required

30–45 minutes

- Exercise: 20–30 minutes
- Debrief: 10–15 minutes

Number of Participants

Two or more groups of 4 to 6

Materials Required

- Precision Delivery Inc. Case Study (from Exercise 3-2)
- PDI Project Proposal (from Exercise 4-3)
- PDI Sampling Data (from Exercise 4-3, electronic format required if participants generate plots and graphs)

- PDI Calculated Data (from Exercise 5-3)

- PDI Basic Plots and Graphs (from Exercise 5-3)

- PDI Dispatch Process Instructions

- New PDI Sampling Data (electronic format required if participants generate plots and graphs)

- New PDI Calculated Data (electronic format required if participants generate plots and graphs)

- Spreadsheet or Statistical Analysis Software (required only if participants generate plots and graphs)

Process

1. Split participants into Project Teams of 4 to 6 people.

2. Give each participant the PDI Case Study, PDI Project Proposal, PDI Sampling Data, PDI Calculated Data, and PDI Basic Plots and Graphs.

3. Tell the groups that as a result of the PDI Six Sigma project a change has been made to the dispatch process and a new set of sample data and related calculations have been generated.

4. Provide each group with the new PDI Dispatch Process Instructions, New PDI Sampling Data, and New PDI Calculated Data (page 200).

5. Ask the groups to review the process change and new data to decide if the project goal has been achieved, if any additional changes should be considered, and which metrics should be tracked to monitor process performance.

6. Debrief the exercise.

Discussion Questions

- How well did the process change work?

- What metrics should be tracked to monitor the process performance?

- What, if any, are the additional improvement opportunities?

Facilitator Notes

Allow additional time if participants are generating new plots and graphs

PDI Dispatch Process Instructions

Step 1: Estimate MPH for a bike based on package weight and for a truck based on facility location and time slot.

- Bike Estimate: MPH = 20 − 0.2(Pounds)

- Truck Estimate:

Time of Day	Downtown	Suburbia
AM	25 MPH	25 MPH
PM	15 MPH	20 MPH

Step 2: Choose the truck only if the estimated speed is more than twice the estimated speed of the bike.

Step 3: Calculate the number of minutes before the customer window to dispatch the bike or truck by using the estimated MPH and the distance to the customer location. Subtract 7.5 to target arrival at the middle of the 15-minute window.

- Minutes Before Window Start = (Miles/MPH) × 60 − 7.5

New PDI Sampling Data

The following data is a systematic sampling of Field Operator trips from downtown (D) or suburban (S) facilities for the first 2 weeks after the dispatch process change and represents roughly 5% of the total sales for that period.

Sample	Week	Day	Facility	Weight (lb.)	Miles (1 Way)	Time Slot	Vehicle	Minutes (1 Way)
1	1	Mon	S	23.3	11.7	AM	Bike	46.1
2	1	Mon	S	44.3	7.4	PM	Bike	39.6
3	1	Mon	S	21.9	0.6	PM	Bike	2.4
4	1	Mon	S	45.5	13.4	AM	Truck	27.0
5	1	Mon	D	33.4	11.3	AM	Bike	50.2
6	1	Tue	S	3.3	11.8	PM	Bike	35.8
7	1	Tue	S	34.5	6.6	PM	Bike	30.9
8	1	Tue	D	41.4	2.9	PM	Bike	14.9
9	1	Tue	D	3.4	2.6	AM	Bike	7.9
10	1	Tue	D	44.2	6.4	AM	Truck	15.0
11	1	Wed	D	20.0	1.8	AM	Bike	6.9
12	1	Wed	S	44.5	9.0	AM	Truck	18.3
13	1	Wed	S	20.6	9.9	AM	Bike	38.5
14	1	Wed	S	47.3	2.4	PM	Bike	14.1
15	1	Wed	S	6.7	1.1	PM	Bike	3.6
16	1	Thu	S	37.4	10.0	AM	Bike	47.5
17	1	Thu	D	21.6	7.1	AM	Bike	28.6
18	1	Thu	S	4.3	7.3	PM	Bike	23.4
19	1	Thu	S	26.7	11.6	AM	Bike	46.9
20	1	Thu	D	4.0	8.9	AM	Bike	27.9
21	1	Fri	D	49.8	13.1	AM	Truck	29.4
22	1	Fri	S	8.7	13.8	AM	Bike	42.2
23	1	Fri	D	16.9	9.0	AM	Bike	33.8
24	1	Fri	D	48.2	9.6	PM	Bike	63.5
25	1	Fri	D	25.8	4.8	AM	Bike	18.1
26	2	Mon	S	17.6	2.3	AM	Bike	8.5
27	2	Mon	D	7.6	2.8	AM	Bike	9.3
28	2	Mon	D	31.1	4.5	AM	Bike	19.6
29	2	Mon	S	11.3	14.1	PM	Bike	47.8
30	2	Mon	S	29.4	4.5	PM	Bike	18.1
31	2	Tue	D	23.7	0.2	PM	Bike	0.8
32	2	Tue	S	11.8	1.9	PM	Bike	6.3
33	2	Tue	S	21.1	4.2	AM	Bike	16.0
34	2	Tue	S	14.4	7.5	AM	Bike	25.6
35	2	Tue	S	10.3	1.9	PM	Bike	6.3
36	2	Wed	D	15.4	7.5	PM	Bike	27.7
37	2	Wed	S	10.2	7.7	AM	Bike	26.2
38	2	Wed	S	38.0	12.2	PM	Bike	62.2
39	2	Wed	D	19.3	5.6	AM	Bike	19.9
40	2	Wed	S	8.5	10.5	PM	Bike	34.6
41	2	Thu	S	18.9	2.8	AM	Bike	10.2
42	2	Thu	D	12.7	14.6	PM	Bike	50.7
43	2	Thu	S	25.3	5.7	AM	Bike	23.0
44	2	Thu	S	17.6	1.8	AM	Bike	6.5
45	2	Thu	S	49.2	4.9	PM	Bike	24.7
46	2	Fri	D	49.7	9.4	PM	Bike	64.5
47	2	Fri	S	44.1	9.5	AM	Truck	19.1
48	2	Fri	D	2.4	13.4	PM	Bike	41.4
49	2	Fri	S	8.7	12.7	PM	Bike	41.9
50	2	Fri	S	18.8	0.0	PM	Bike	0.1

New PDI Calculated Data

Sample	MPH	Fld Op ($)[1]	Idle Mins[2]	Idle ($)	Revenue ($)	Rebate ($)	Margin ($)	USL[3]	LSL[4]	IN/OUT
1	15.3	11.53	0.00	0.00	28.32	0.00	16.79	53	38	IN
2	11.3	9.90	0.00	0.00	49.33	0.00	39.42	48	33	IN
3	16.4	0.59	0.00	0.00	26.94	0.00	26.34	15	0	IN
4	29.7	13.50	0.00	0.00	50.52	0.00	37.02	40	25	IN
5	13.5	12.54	0.00	0.00	38.41	0.00	25.87	58	43	IN
6	19.8	8.96	0.00	0.00	8.32	0.00	-0.64	44	29	IN
7	12.9	7.71	0.00	0.00	39.45	0.00	31.74	38	23	IN
8	11.8	3.73	0.00	0.00	46.37	0.00	42.64	23	8	IN
9	19.3	1.98	0.00	0.00	8.44	0.00	6.46	15	0	IN
10	25.5	7.50	0.00	0.00	49.15	0.00	41.66	23	8	IN
11	16.0	1.71	0.00	0.00	24.98	0.00	23.27	15	0	IN
12	29.5	9.16	0.00	0.00	49.46	0.00	40.30	29	14	IN
13	15.4	9.63	0.00	0.00	25.59	0.00	15.96	45	30	IN
14	10.2	3.54	0.00	0.00	52.32	0.00	48.78	21	6	IN
15	18.9	0.91	0.00	0.00	11.69	0.00	10.78	15	0	IN
16	12.7	11.88	0.00	0.00	42.37	0.00	30.49	56	41	IN
17	14.9	7.15	0.00	0.00	26.59	0.00	19.44	35	20	IN
18	18.8	5.84	0.00	0.00	9.34	0.00	3.49	30	15	IN
19	14.8	11.72	0.00	0.00	31.74	0.00	20.02	55	40	IN
20	19.2	6.98	0.00	0.00	9.00	0.00	2.02	35	20	IN
21	26.7	14.70	0.00	0.00	54.81	0.00	40.10	39	24	IN
22	19.6	10.55	0.00	0.00	13.68	0.00	3.13	53	38	IN
23	16.1	8.44	0.00	0.00	21.94	0.00	13.49	40	25	IN
24	9.1	15.88	0.00	0.00	53.20	53.20	-15.88	63	48	OUT
25	15.8	4.52	0.00	0.00	30.82	0.00	26.30	27	12	IN
26	16.4	2.14	0.00	0.00	22.61	0.00	20.47	16	1	IN
27	18.2	2.32	0.00	0.00	12.58	0.00	10.26	17	2	IN
28	13.7	4.90	0.00	0.00	36.09	0.00	31.18	27	12	IN
29	17.6	11.95	0.00	0.00	16.28	0.00	4.33	55	40	IN
30	14.9	4.53	0.00	0.00	34.35	0.00	29.82	27	12	IN
31	15.6	0.20	0.00	0.00	28.69	0.00	28.49	15	0	IN
32	18.1	1.57	0.00	0.00	16.80	0.00	15.22	15	0	IN
33	15.7	3.99	0.00	0.00	26.13	0.00	22.14	23	8	IN
34	17.6	6.39	0.00	0.00	19.41	0.00	13.02	34	19	IN
35	17.9	1.57	0.00	0.00	15.26	0.00	13.69	15	0	IN
36	16.3	6.93	0.00	0.00	20.44	0.00	13.51	34	19	IN
37	17.6	6.56	0.00	0.00	15.15	0.00	8.60	33	18	IN
38	11.8	15.56	0.00	0.00	42.98	0.00	27.42	67	52	IN
39	16.8	4.97	0.00	0.00	24.31	0.00	19.35	28	13	IN
40	18.1	8.66	0.00	0.00	13.47	0.00	4.81	42	27	IN
41	16.4	2.55	0.00	0.00	23.94	0.00	21.39	18	3	IN
42	17.3	12.69	0.00	0.00	17.66	0.00	4.98	58	43	IN
43	14.9	5.76	0.00	0.00	30.29	0.00	24.53	31	16	IN
44	16.9	1.63	0.00	0.00	22.59	0.00	20.96	15	0	IN
45	11.9	6.18	0.00	0.00	54.22	0.00	48.03	37	22	IN
46	8.7	16.12	0.00	0.00	54.72	54.72	-16.12	63	48	OUT
47	29.9	9.56	0.00	0.00	49.05	0.00	39.49	30	15	IN
48	19.4	10.34	0.00	0.00	7.37	0.00	-2.97	49	34	IN
49	18.1	10.47	0.00	0.00	13.66	0.00	3.19	49	34	IN
50	15.9	0.02	0.00	0.00	23.82	0.00	23.80	15	0	IN

[1]Fld Op ($) = Field Operations Dollars; [2]Idle Mins = Idle Minutes; [3]USL = Upper Specification Limit; [4]LSL = Lower Specification Limit

Chapter Eight

Will There Be a Change Reaction?
Dealing with Resistance

Six Sigma projects drive change in organizations. Successful initial implementation of process changes and maintenance of the momentum of positive process changes requires overcoming resistance to change. These exercises will help participants understand and recognize resistance to change and develop skills to manage change effectively.

EXERCISE 8-1

Changing Seats (Resistance to Change)

Description

A quick and easy game where participants are asked to change where they are sitting so they can experience the emotions and feelings often associated with change.

Purpose

■ Increase participant understanding of the emotional barriers to resistance and how to deal with them

■ Increase participant understanding of the support needed to keep changes in place

Time Required

5 to 15 minutes, depending on debrief

Number of Participants

Unlimited

Materials Required

None

Process

At some point during the training ask participants to change seats.

Discussion Questions

■ How did it feel to be asked to change seats?

■ Did you view changing seats as an opportunity to sit with someone new or as an uncomfortable or undesirable change?

■ What are some things that make people resistant to change?

■ What can you do to make it easier for people in your organizations to accept the changes associated with Six Sigma?

If participants move back to their old seating arrangements after the exercise is over, ask the following questions:

■ Why is it difficult to maintain changes once they are made?

■ What kind of support is necessary to maintain the changes associated with Six Sigma?

Facilitator Notes

- Encourage participants to consider and share their own personal emotions related to making changes. This is what makes this exercise powerful.

- As an optional approach, you can ask participants to change seats without a debriefing. Then, after they have become comfortable in their new seats, ask them to change seats again, this time following up with the debriefing.

- Asking participants to change seats frequently can also help them enhance their personal ability to deal with change.

EXERCISE 8-2

Personal Appearance Change Challenge (Understanding Resistance to Change)

Description

Participants make changes to their personal appearance so they can experience the emotions and feelings often associated with change.

Purpose

- Increase participant understanding of the emotional barriers to resistance and how to deal with them

- Increase participant understanding of the support needed to keep changes in place

Time Required

30 minutes

Number of Participants

Pairs of 2

Materials Required

None

Process

1. Tell participants they are going to participate in an experiment about making changes. Ask them if they will agree to live with the changes made until the experiment is over. Let them know this experiment takes about 30 minutes and they won't have to make any changes they feel uncomfortable with.

2. Have participants choose a partner and stand facing their partners.

3. Ask them to study their partner because the partner will be making some changes.

4. Have one participant from each pair turn their back to their partner and make 5 changes to their physical appearance (move their watch from one wrist to another, remove a shoe, remove their glasses, etc.). Ask the other partner to close their eyes.

5. Give participants 30 seconds to complete the changes.

6. Have participants face each other again, all eyes open, and ask the partner who did not make changes to identify as many changes as possible. (Allow about 30 seconds for this.)

7. Do 2 more rounds of steps 4 to 6.

8. Finally, ask participants to make 10 changes in 20 seconds. (You will likely get some resistance at this point). When you

start to get verbal resistance stop and move on to the discussion questions.

Discussion Questions

- How did it feel to be asked to make so many changes?

- What are some things that make people resistant to change?

- What can you do to make it easier for people in your organizations to accept the changes associated with Six Sigma?

Begin with the preceding questions. At some point participants will begin to reverse the changes made during the exercise. When this starts to happen ask the following questions:

- Why is it difficult to maintain changes once they are made?

- What kind of support is necessary to maintain the changes associated with Six Sigma?

Facilitator Notes

- During the setup of the exercise, make sure the participants agree they will maintain whatever changes are made until the exercise is over.

- Encourage participants to consider and share their own personal emotions related to making changes. This is what makes this exercise powerful.

- Some participants may make the point that these changes are not like changes being made in the organization. If this happens, acknowledge the validity of the statement, but ask how these changes, and people's reactions to them, are similar.

EXERCISE 8-3

Change Champion (Getting "Buy-In" to Change)

Description

In this game a designated leader must convince his or her
followers to eat an unknown substance.

Purpose

- Demonstrate the dynamics of resistance to change

- Examine methods to overcome resistance to change

- Allow participants to explore the emotional issues
  associated with change

Time Required

30 minutes

Number of Participants

Groups of 5 to 7

Materials Required

- Bowl with cover

- Spoons

- Unappetizing food substance (see Facilitator Notes, page 208)

Process

1. Arrange participants into groups of 5 to 7.

2. Ask each group to select a change leader.

3. Take the leaders out of the room.

4. Provide each leader with a covered bowl. The cover should obscure the substance so it cannot be seen.

5. Provide leaders with spoons for all members of their group, including themselves.

6. Tell the leaders: "The change you are championing requires 2 levels of commitment. First, you must get everyone on your team to agree to eat 1 spoonful of whatever is in this bowl, sight unseen. Second, after you have unanimous consent, all team members must follow through on their commitment and eat their spoonful. Any questions?"

7. Answer any questions and give participants a few moments to devise their change strategies while you go back inside the room and brief the "followers."

8. Tell followers that their leaders will try to convince them to accept a change and they should react to it as they would under any normal circumstance.

9. Bring the leaders back into the room and let them work with their group.

10. Allow about 10 minutes and then proceed to debrief.

Discussion Questions

■ For Leaders

  ■ What strategies did you use to get your team to commit to eating the food?

  ■ Did you use any different strategies to get them to actually eat the food?

  ■ From your perspective, what worked and what didn't?

■ For Followers

  ■ What did your leader do that was effective in convincing you to eat the food?

■ What did your leader do to discourage you from eating?

■ Was it harder to follow through on your commitment to eat the food than it was to make the commitment?

■ For All

■ How is accepting the changes recommended by a Six Sigma project like asking someone to eat an unknown substance?

■ What approaches might be effective in getting people to accept and commit to the changes?

Facilitator Notes

■ Leaders use a variety of tactics to gain buy-in including lying ("I know what's in the bowl and it's just fine to eat.") or volunteering to go first. Some might even resist trying to get buy-in from their followers because they don't know what's in the bowl and so don't know if it's good for the followers. Whatever they do, their behaviors relate well to dealing with change and acceptance on a Six Sigma project.

■ The substance in the bowl should be something that looks unappetizing, but is perfectly safe to eat. Yogurt with some food coloring in it to make it a strange color works well.

EXERCISE 8-4

Paper Animals (Reactions to Change)

Description

This is a fun and energetic exercise where participants have an opportunity to demonstrate how they deal with change in real time. Participants work in groups to create animal shapes out of newspaper to a set of criteria and then must deal with a change in the criteria.

Purpose

- Energize participants through an experiential exercise that relates to their work experiences

- Allow participants to practice effective teamwork behaviors (planning, communication, identification of roles, leadership, etc.) while accomplishing a task with an ambiguous goal

- Explore the dynamics of dealing with change

Time Required

- 30 minutes for setup and exercise
- 30 minutes for debrief

Materials

- Newspaper (about a 1-foot-high stack for each team)
- Masking tape (a roll for each team)
- String (a roll for each team)
- Scissors (a pair for each team)
- Prizes, if desired
- Observer worksheets

Number of Participants

10 to 100 or more

Process

1. Break participants into groups of 10 or fewer.

2. Ask each team to select an observer. (Give observers instruction sheets.)

3. Explain the task is to build an animal with the materials provided: newspaper, tape, string, scissors. Tell them the groups are in competition with each other. The criteria for the winning animal are:

   ■ Structural integrity (the animal must be freestanding and sturdy)

   ■ Anatomical accuracy (the animal should be readily recognizable)

4. Tell the teams they have 25 minutes to complete their animals. Have them begin.

5. After teams have been working for 10 minutes, add the criteria that the animals will also be judged on how tall they are.

6. Tell them the winning team will now be judged by a group voting process (each group gets a single vote).

7. After 25 minutes, cut off activity.

8. Ask groups to clean up their areas.

9. Give the groups 5 minutes to look at the animals produced by the other groups and 10 minues to meet as a group and decide which animal to vote for.

10. Tally votes, announce winner.

Discussion Questions

Debrief in small groups. Start with the observer's comments and then open up the discussion to the group. Each small group should identify at least 3 key learnings or observations to share with the whole group.

- What did the teams do well?

- What could the teams have done better?

- Did teams have a common vision at start of implementation? At any time?

- Were everyone's ideas and inputs considered?

- Did the team respond effectively to the change in criteria?

- How different would your animal have looked if you had all 3 criteria at the beginning of exercise? What is it that stopped you from creating that animal?

- How was the team in this exercise similar or different from your team(s) back on the job?

- How effective were you personally?

Facilitator Notes

- When discussing how the teams responded to the change, encourage the teams to explore how they felt about the change. Did they view it as a problem (fairness is often mentioned as an issue) or as a challenge to respond to?

- Common reactions to the change in criteria are:

  - Do nothing different

  - Redesign (sometimes creating a whole new animal)

  - Make small, easily implemented changes to the original design

- Respondents usually say that their animal would have been quite different had they had all 3 criteria at the beginning of the exercise. Many note they would have selected a different animal to create (giraffe, bear, etc.). This issue brings out many of the dynamics of change (fear that they didn't have time to start over on a new animal, reluctance to waste the work done so far, resistance to making another group decision, etc.).

Paper Animals Exercise Observer's Worksheet

These questions are issues to look for. You do not have to answer each.

1. Did the group start with an effective plan? Were all alternatives considered?

2. How effectively did the group define or identify potential problems?

3. How did the group react to the change in criteria?

4. Did the group make significant changes to the animal based on the change in criteria? How were they able to adjust or why did they not?

5. Were ideas communicated clearly? How well did the group members listen to each other?

6. Were the group's tasks, resources, and roles clear to each group member?

7. What process did the group use to decide which animal they would vote for?

EXERCISE 8-5

Island Dance (Managing the Fear of Change)

Description

Participants must maintain a "safe" position in a rope ring while the number of safe opportunities (rings) continually decreases.

Purpose

- Explore emotional and behavioral reactions to threatening change

- Explore how process changes from a Six Sigma project can affect teamwork

Time Required

- Exercise: 15 minutes

- Debrief: 15 minutes

Number of Participants

20 to 100

Materials Required

- Rope circles in a variety of sizes. Some should be so small as to accommodate only a single person standing in it, while a single circle must be large enough to accommodate the feet of all the participants. The key is that this circle must not be large enough to accommodate all participants *easily*. Many participants should have to get their feet in the largest circle by sitting on the floor and placing just their feet, not their bodies, in the circle.

■ An open space large enough to allow all of the participants to move freely.

Process

1. Lay the circles out on the floor.

2. Tell participants that the circles represent islands of organizational safety. To be safe participants must have their feet completely within a circle.

3. Have participants stand up and place themselves in a circle.

4. Tell them when you yell, "Process change!" they must move to a different circle than the circle they are currently in.

5. Yell, "Process change."

6. After participants have repositioned themselves, yell, "Process change" again and remove 1 or 2 of the circles from the floor.

7. Do this a few times until only a few of the large circles are left.

8. The last time you yell, "Process change" take up all of the circles but the largest circle, forcing all participants into that circle to remain "safe."

9. Proceed to debrief.

Discussion Questions

■ How did people behave when it became apparent that there might not be enough "safe" space for everyone?

■ How did it feel when someone helped or hindered you in your quest for "safe" space?

■ Did pressure spark creative solutions or destructive competition?

- How can you keep people focused on team versus individual success?

- Why might your Six Sigma projects be perceived as a threat by those in the organization?

- What can you do to make them less threatening?

Facilitator Notes

- The number of circles required at the start can vary with the size of the group, but 10 to 15 circles is a good guideline.

- The exercise is designed to create the appearance that there will not be enough safe spots for everyone. Some participants will act in a "survival mode"—thinking only of their own safety, while others will take a "team" approach and work to ensure that everyone is safe.

- Some "breakthrough" thinking is required for everyone to end up with a safe spot. The breakthrough is to realize that people do not need to be standing up to have both feet in a circle. By sitting and placing just their feet in a circle, many more people can fit than if they were standing up. If participants do not come to the breakthrough on their own, give them some hints. Everyone should end up safe at the end of the exercise.

Chapter Nine

Is Our Team Geared for Success?
Team Behaviors

Successful Six Sigma project teams require effective teamwork between project members. These exercises will help participants with the issues of defining a common definition of success (goal setting) and defining team behaviors regarding how they will work together.

EXERCISE 9-1
Clue (Team versus Individual Goals)

Description

This is a problem-solving exercise reminiscent of a popular board game in which participants must work together to solve a mystery.

Purpose

- Explore the issue of competitive versus cooperative behavior in teams

■ Explore how individual goals versus team goals can affect team effectiveness

Time Required

30 minutes

Number of participants

10 to 50

Materials Required

Clue sheets (each clue sheet must have the entire preamble in addition to a single clue or several clues. For groups of 13 or more participants (there are 13 clues) a single clue per sheet is appropriate. Smaller groups require that some participants receive more than a single clue sheet or that multiple clues are included on a single sheet. All of the clues should be disseminated for the exercise.

Preamble

■ A murder has taken place to which there were no witnesses.

■ Your objective: Determine who did it, in which room, and with which weapon.

The Suspects

Mrs. Peacock

Col. Mustard

Mrs. White

Ms. Scarlet

Prof. Plum

Rev. Green

The Locations

Hall

Dining Room

Kitchen

Conservatory

Billiard Room

Library

The Weapons

Knife

Candlestick

Wrench

Rope

Lead Pipe

Revolver

The Clues

When the murder occurred:

1. Mrs. Peacock was in the kitchen.

2. Mrs. White was in the library.

3. Rev. Green was in the library.

4. Col. Mustard was in the kitchen.

5. Mrs. Scarlet was in the billiard room.

6. The murder did not occur in the billiard room.

7. Prof. Plum was not in the conservatory.

8. The murder did not occur in the dining room.

9. The knife was in the kitchen.

10. Col. Mustard had the revolver.

11. The lead pipe was in the library.

12. Ms. Scarlet had the rope.

13. Rev. Green was using the wrench.

Process

1. Distribute a clue sheet to each participant. Make sure all 13 clues are distributed.

2. Read the preamble aloud. Tell participants that each person has either a single clue or several clues that will help solve the mystery and that they have 15 minutes to exchange information with others.

3. Instruct them to tell the facilitator when they believe they have the correct answer.

4. The exercise is complete when someone correctly solves the mystery.

5. Offer a prize for the first person to solve the mystery.

6. Start the exercise. Give a time reminder when 5 minutes are left and every minute thereafter.

7. When someone has arrived at the correct answer, stop the exercise and proceed to the discussion questions.

Discussion Questions

- Do participants openly share information?

- Do participants engage in negotiation tactics to increase their own information while limiting others?

- Do participants give false information to others?

- How did the prize incentive affect behavior?

- Was the goal perceived as an individual or team goal? Why?

- What can your project do to avoid destructive, competitive team behaviors?

Facilitator Notes

- Solution: Professor Plum, in the hall, with the candlestick.

- The prize emphasizes the potential competitive nature of this exercise and may bring out behaviors that affect team effectiveness.

- Participants often perceive the objective as an individual goal, even though that is never stated.

- The prize for the first person to solve the mystery can represent individually based incentive systems present in many organizations.

Exercise 9-2

Balloon Sculpture Exercise (Defining Goals with Ambiguous Metrics)

Description

In this team-building exercise participants must work together to build a "work of art" from balloons.

Purpose

- Allow participants to practice defining and accomplishing clear, actionable team goals while working with subjective measures of success

- Allow participants to experience the impacts of common goal definitions on team outcomes

Time Required

1 hour

- 35 minutes for setup and exercise

- 25 minutes for debrief

Materials

- Balloons (60 to 100 per team)

- A roll of masking tape for each team

- Prizes, if desired

- Observer worksheets

Number of Participants

10 to 50

Process

1. Select an observer for each team. (Give observers instruction sheets.)

2. Break remaining participants into teams of 3 to 7.

3. Explain the task is to create an artistic sculpture using the materials provided: balloons and tape.

4. The teams have 10 minutes to plan how they will create their sculpture. The planning phase will be followed by a 15-minute implementation phase.

5. The teams are in competition with each other. The winning sculpture will be decided through a voting process.

6. Check for questions and begin the planning period.

7. After 10 minutes, start the implementation phase. After 15 minutes, stop activity.

8. Give teams 5 minutes to look at sculptures and meet as a team and decide which sculpture to vote for.

9. Tally votes, announce winner, and award prizes, if available.

Discussion Questions

- Debrief in teams. Start with observer comments and open up the discussion to the team. Each team should identify at least 3 key learnings or observations to share with the whole group (approximately 20 minutes).

- Bring all of the teams together and share key learnings or observations (approximately 5 minutes).

Facilitator Notes

- Make sure the balloons you provide are easy to blow up. Test a few before the exercise.

■ Avoid the small, "water balloon" type of balloons, but a variety of sizes and shapes can be used.

Balloon Sculpture Exercise Observer's Worksheet

1. Did the team start with a clearly defined goal? Was the goal clearly defined at any time?

    _____

2. Did the team start with an effective plan? Were several alternatives considered?

    _____

3. How effectively did the team define or identify potential problems?

    _____

4. Were ideas communicated clearly? Were everyone's ideas and inputs considered?

    _____

5. How did the teams handle time pressure?

    _____

6. Were the team's tasks and roles clear to each team member?

    _____

7. What process did the team use to decide which sculpture they would vote for?

    _____

EXERCISE 9-3

4 Suits, 5 Hands (Exploring Team Behaviors)

Description

In this exercise participants are required to work together with restrictive work rules to achieve a challenging task.

Purpose

- Examine team behaviors and emotions in a challenging and tightly structured environment
- Explore the issue of individual goals versus team goals

Time Required

25 to 30 minutes

- Exercise: 10–15 minutes
- Debrief: 15 minutes

Number of Participants

Teams of 4 plus an observer

Materials Required

- Playing Cards (1 deck per team)
- Observer sheets

Process

1. Select volunteers to act as observers.

2. Divide participants into teams of 4 people.

3. Assign an observer to each team. A single observer may observe multiple teams.

4. Explain the objectives and procedures to participants:

   ■ Each team will receive 25 cards.

   ■ Each team member will receive all of the cards of a particular suit.

   ■ The team objective is to create 5 "pat" hands from their 25 cards.

   ■ A *pat hand* consists of 5 cards that make a flush (all the same suit); a straight (unbroken sequence); a full-house (3 of a kind plus a pair); or a hand containing 4 of a kind.

   ■ There will be 5 piles of cards. One pile in front of each team member and another pile in the middle of the table. The objective is achieved when each pile is a pat hand of 5 cards.

   ■ Team members may touch only those cards directly in front of them or in the middle of the table.

   ■ Team members may put cards in or take cards out of the middle pile.

   ■ The remaining stack of cards from the deck will be placed (face down) in the middle of the table. Any team member may remove a card from the middle pile and replace it with a card from the top of the deck. This is usually not necessary to complete the task.

   ■ No talking or gesturing is allowed during the exercise.

5. Have observers select 25 cards at random from the deck and separate them by the 4 suits.

6. Have observers give all the cards from a single suit to each of the team members. (In the unlikely event there are no cards from one or more suits, then one or more team members will start with no cards.)

7. Tell participants to inform the facilitator when they have met their objective.

Discussion Questions

Start with comments from the observers. Then discuss the following with all participants:

■ Was it difficult to keep the team goal in mind (i.e., 5 pat hands)?

■ What was frustrating about this exercise?

■ How is this similar to getting work done on your project?

■ What team behaviors or team "ground rules" would help in this situation?

Facilitator Notes

■ The key to completing this exercise successfully is having participants who are willing to break up a pat hand in front of them to help complete the hand in the middle of the table.

■ Five pat hands can almost always be created from 25 randomly selected cards. You may want to practice this yourself before running the exercise.

4 Suits, 5 Hands Observer's Sheet

Your role is to observe and help enforce the rules of the exercise.

Rules

- No talking or gesturing.

- Team members may touch only those cards directly in front of them or in the middle of the table.

- Team members may put cards in or take cards out of the middle pile.

- The remaining stack of cards from the deck will be placed (face down) in the middle of the table. Any team member may remove a card from the middle pile and replace it with a card from the top of the deck. This is usually not necessary to complete the task.

Observation Questions

- Are people willing to give away cards from the piles directly in front of them?

- Did anyone get a pat hand in front of himself or herself and then withdraw from the group problem-solving process?

- What is the level of frustration?

- Is everyone involved in accomplishing the team goal (i.e., 5 pat hands)?

EXERCISE 9-4

I Want to Drive (Setting Common Expectations)

Description

Team members use the scenario of a teenager and parent negotiating driving privileges to practice setting common expectations.

Purpose

- Explore the two-way nature of relationships
- Teach participants to align expectations with other team members

Time Required

60 minutes

- 5 minutes for setup
- 30 minutes for role play
- 25 minutes for debrief

Number of Participants

Participants work in pairs

Materials Required

Agreements Worksheet

Process

1. Arrange participants in pairs. Provide each person with an Agreements Worksheet.

2. Explain to participants that they will be participating in a role-playing exercise. One of them will be a teenager who

wants to learn how to drive. The other will be the teenager's parent. Ask each pair to select who will play each role.

3. Ask participants to draft a personal success statement on their worksheet. Give them up to 5 minutes if needed.

4. Participants should then review their partner's statement. They may ask for clarifications, but they are not allowed to suggest revisions.

5. When they have completed their reviews, have them complete the commitment and expectations statements. Give them up to 5 minutes.

6. Ask participants to take turns responding to their partner's expectations statements. Tell them they can respond to each expectation statement with, "I will," "I will if..." or "I will not because...."

7. Have them modify their expectations statements if necessary until both the parent and teenager have come to an agreement on expectations of the other or time has run out. Allow 20 minutes for negotiations.

Discussion Questions

Have participants take turns discussing the following questions in their pairs. Ask each pair to identify 3 ways to negotiate effective team relationships (15 minutes):

■ Were the success statements clear?

■ Did knowing your partners success statement help you come to agreement on expectations? Why or why not?

■ Were the expectations initially reasonable?

■ Did your negotiations help you better understand your partner's point of view?

■ Did you attempt to create balance between what you committed to and what you expected from the other person?

- What hindered negotiations?
- What helped negotiations?

Have each pair share the 3 ways they identified to negotiate effective team relationships (10 minutes).

Facilitator Notes

- This game requires little from the facilitator beyond the setup.
- If you have many pairs of participants, to save time, you can ask each pair to share only a single "lesson learned" with the whole group.

I Want to Drive Agreements Worksheet

Personal Success Statement

I will consider this negotiation a personal success if I ...

_____

_____

_____

Commitment Statement

To achieve my success statement, I will ...

_____

_____

_____

Expectations Statement

To help me achieve my success statement, I expect you to ...

_____

_____

_____

Chapter Ten

How Do We Stay on Track?
Project Management

Six Sigma requires effective planning, organizing, and communication. The exercises in this chapter will help participants build strong project management and project team behaviors that will create and maintain momentum behind their Six Sigma efforts.

EXERCISE 10-1
Camel by Committee (Integrating Project Teams)

Description

This exercise explores the dynamics project teams face in coordinating and integrating the efforts of multiple subteams working to accomplish a complex task. It simulates the planning, construct/build, and integration phases common to most projects, including the physical and organizational barriers that are often present. It also produces a symbolic touchstone that the team can refer to throughout the life of the project.

Purpose

Explore project management issues, including:

- Communications
- Organization structure
- Planning
- Implementation

Time Required

- Exercise: 35 minutes
- Debrief: 25 minutes

Number of Participants

10–100

Materials Required

- Stacks of newspaper
- Masking tape

Process

1. Divide participants into subteams by function. Explain the objectives and procedures to participants.

2. The team objective is to build a 3-dimensional figure of a camel.

3. Each subteam will be responsible for 1 of the following components. (If you have fewer than 5 subteams, you can combine neck with head and tail with body. Another option is to have a separate integration team. This would represent the project management team.)

- Head

- Legs and feet

- Humps

- Body

- Neck and tail

4. There are 3 phases: planning, construct/build, and integration.

   - The time allotted for planning is 5 minutes. During the planning phase all team members may communicate freely. The team should allocate materials to each subteam during this phase.

   - The construct/build phase is 15 minutes. During this phase subteams will separate physically and may only communicate with each other in writing. The facilitator will convey messages. Sharing of materials is allowed, but not explicitly explained. (If an integration team is used they can communicate with all subteams. No other communication is permitted.)

   - The integration phase is 10 minutes. All team members may interact freely during this period.

Discussion Questions

Debrief in subteams first around the following questions:

- Was your subteam effective? Why?

- How could you have been more effective?

Debrief the entire team using the following questions:

- How did the organization structure, timing for each phase, and resource distribution affect the project outcome?

- What were similarities to the way we manage projects?

- Did the team communicate effectively or ineffectively? Why?

- Did the team have an effective plan and commonly understood vision of the outcome?

- Did the team make good use of all of its resources?

- How were decisions made?

- Did the team share equally in the outcome?

- What would have made the team more effective?

Facilitator Notes

- This is a relatively easy game to facilitate and debrief. Relationships between the results of this game and participants' efforts on the job are usually readily apparent.

- One of the keys to producing something that actually resembles a camel is if teams address the issue of scale early on. If all the subteams have a common concept of the scale of the finished product, they are likely to have greater success.

- How you play the role of messenger during the implementation phase can affect the game's learning points. You can alertly and quickly convey messages between teams or act as a slow or defective e-mail system. If you choose to convey messages slowly (or even lose messages), be sure to focus the debrief on how participants reacted to the poor messaging. Don't let them focus on blaming the facilitator for their results.

- Encourage the team to keep their "camel" as a symbol for their project team and as a reminder of the lessons learned.

EXERCISE 10-2

Domino Designs (Building an Effective Project Team)

Description

This exercise simulates the project team environment by having participants create a pattern of dominoes while working in a project team structure.

Purpose

Explore communication, planning, and implementation issues, particularly with functionally separated project teams.

Time Required

- Exercise: 35 minutes
- Debrief: 25 minutes

Number of Participants

10 to 50

Materials Required

- Dominoes (approximately 50 per person)
- Large, flat surface for placing dominoes (A floor with a smooth, hard surface is most appropriate for this exercise.)

Process

1. Divide participants into subteams of 4 to 6.

2. Explain the objectives and procedures to participants:

- The team objective is to use all of the dominoes provided to build a single pattern of dominoes standing on end so that when 1 domino is tipped over all will follow in turn.

- Each subteam is responsible for placing its own dominoes.

- There are 2 phases: planning and implementation.

- The time allotted for planning is 10 minutes. During the planning phase all team members may communicate freely.

- The implementation phase is 10 minutes.

- Each subteam will select a project lead. During the implementation phase only project leads may communicate with one another.

- No other communication is allowed between subteams. Subteam members may communicate freely within their subteam.

3. Provide an equal number of dominoes to each subteam. (If some teams are larger than others then some teams will have more/less dominoes per person.)

4. Start the planning phase.

5. After 10 minutes start the implementation phase.

6. Allow time for the placement of all of the dominoes.

7. When all dominoes have been set, ask for a volunteer to test whether the team met the objective by knocking over the first domino in the design.

Discussion Questions

Debrief in the large group around the following questions:

- Did the team have an effective plan and commonly understood vision of the outcome?

- Did each person and subteam have a clearly defined role?

- Did the team make good use of all of its resources?

- How were decisions made?

- How did the project communication restrictions affect the outcome?

- What would have made the team more effective?

- What were the similarities to Six Sigma projects you have worked on?

Facilitator Notes

- If this exercise is being run with a large, intact Six Sigma project team, arrange participants into subgroups by function, if appropriate.

- If you have participants who are physically unable to place dominoes, they can still be a member of a subteam assisting with planning, encouraging, organizing, etc., or they can play an observer role.

EXERCISE 10-3

Team Theatre (Effective Teamwork)

Description

This game is a light-hearted, energetic, fun activity in which participants work together to script and perform a version of a well-known movie.

Purpose

- Encourage interaction among team members

- Break down barriers to open communication

- Encourage behavior outside of normal comfort zones

- Have fun

- Explore issues of planning, time pressure, decision making, role clarity, and communication

Time Required

45 to 90 minutes depending on the number of teams

Number of Participants

Groups of 20 to 50

Process

1. Share the name of the activity and its objectives.

2. Break the group into teams of roughly equal size. Limit team size to 10 participants.

3. Announce: "Each team must plan, script, and perform a 5-minute version of the movie that I am about to assign to you. Your team may reject the first movie you are given, but if you do, you must perform the second movie. You cannot default back to the first movie."

4. Assign each team a movie. The movies should be generally well known. Some examples:

   Wizard of Oz

   Sound of Music

   Cinderella

   Ten Commandments

   West Side Story

   Adventures of Robin Hood

It's a Wonderful Life

A Christmas Carol

Rocky Horror Picture Show

Star Wars

5. Allow 15 minutes for planning.

6. Teams take turns performing for the other teams.

Discussion Questions

■ Did the group come to clear agreement on an implementation plan?

■ How did the group assign roles?

■ How did the group make decisions?

■ What about this exercise was particularly challenging?

■ Did your group make effective use of the time allotted for planning and performing? Why or why not?

■ How was team behavior in this exercise similar or dissimilar to your Six Sigma projects?

Facilitator Notes

■ Create a list of movies prior to the activity. The list should include 2 movies for each team in case all teams reject their first choice.

■ Establish the order in which teams present ahead of time as this can be a topic of contention.

■ If some participants are not familiar with the movie their team has selected, encourage them to fully participate and rely on their teammates for help.

EXERCISE 10-4

Draw It (Communicating Effectively)

Description

Participants sit back-to-back and attempt to replicate a simple drawing through verbal instructions.

Purpose

- Teach participants the importance of active listening
- Allow participants to practice effective communication behaviors
- Explore the differences between 1-way and 2-way communication

Time Required

1 hour

- 5 minutes for setup and instructions
- 15 minutes to complete and review diagram 1
- 15 minutes to complete and review diagram 2
- 25 minutes for debrief

Number of Participants

2 to 50, limited by logistics

Materials Required

- Writing instruments
- Blank paper for drawing
- A copy of diagrams 1 and 2 for each pair of participants

Process

1. Arrange participants into pairs. If there are an odd number of participants, allow a group of 3.

2. Have 1 person in each pair or trio volunteer to be the "speaker." The remaining person or persons are the "listeners." Have the speakers arrange their chairs so they sit back-to-back with the listeners.

3. Provide each speaker with a copy of diagram 1 and ensure each listener has paper and a writing instrument. Make sure the listeners do not see the diagram.

4. Address the group as follows: "The speakers are going to describe a diagram to their listeners. Based on their description, the listeners are to re-create the diagram on their paper. Listeners are not allowed to speak or make any other noise."

5. Ask the speakers to describe their diagram to their listener. Remind listeners not to make any noise. Tell them they have 12 minutes to complete their diagrams.

6. After 12 minutes, ask listeners to compare their diagram with the diagram of the speaker. If pairs finish their diagrams early, they may start this process as soon as they have finished.

7. After pairs have had a couple of minutes to compare their diagrams, ask them to set aside their diagrams and take their back-to-back positions again.

8. Tell them they will try to re-create another diagram, but this time the listener may ask questions of the speaker during the exercise.

9. Hand out diagram 2 and ask the pairs to begin.

10. After 12 minutes, ask listeners to compare their diagram with the diagram of the speaker. If pairs finish their

diagrams early, they may start this process as soon as they have finished.

Discussion Questions

Debrief as a group using the questions below. The theme to draw out is the impact of active listening on the speaker and listener and its impact on the effectiveness of communications. (Allow approximately 25 minutes.)

- How did the speakers feel while giving instructions on diagram 1? How did the speakers feel while giving instructions on diagram 2?

- How did the listeners feel while receiving instructions on diagram 1? How did the listeners feel while receiving instructions on diagram 2?

- How did the re-creations of diagram 1 compare to diagram 2?

- What are the advantages and disadvantages of 1-way communication (passive listening)?

- What are the advantages and disadvantages of 2-way communication (active listening)?

Facilitator Notes

- You can run this exercise with different drawings if desired. A more complex drawing can be used to bring out discussion relevant to a very complex Six Sigma project.

- This exercise can also be used as a learning tool for Operational Definitions (debrief on defining common language).

Draw It—Diagram 1

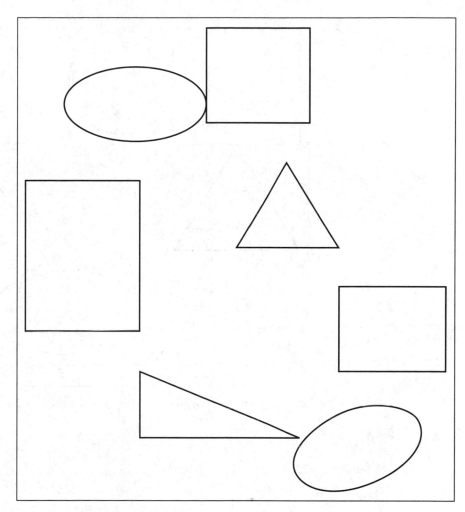

Figure 10.1   Draw It—Diagram 1

Draw It—Diagram 2

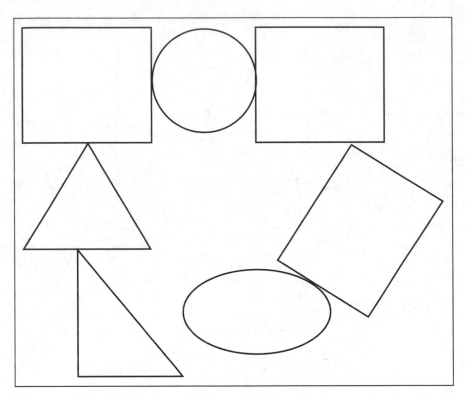

Figure 10.2   Draw It—Diagram 2

INDEX

*Main entries for game exercises are listed in **bold**.*